Write Better and Get Ahead at Work

Write Better and Get Ahead at Work

Successful methods for writing the easy, natural way

Michael Dolan

Writers Club Press
San Jose New York Lincoln Shanghai

Write Better and Get Ahead at Work
Successful methods for writing the easy, natural way

Writers Club Press
an imprint of iUniverse.com, Inc.

For information address:
iUniverse.com, Inc.
620 North 48th Street, Suite 201
Lincoln, NE 68504-3467
www.iuniverse.com

ISBN: 0-595-12019-9

Printed in the United States of America

*To all the **Writing for Action** seminar participants*
who made me stop and think.

Featuring Favorite New Yorker cartoons

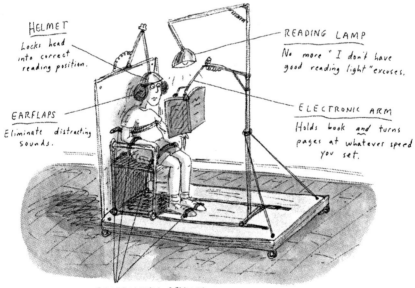

Contents

If Possible, Substitute "Since" or" Because" for "As."
The Right Form of the Possessive, or Where does the Apostrophe Go?
  Other Uses of the Apostrophe
Contract Words to Sound More Personal.
Correct: 8 p.m. and 8:15 p.m. or 8 P.M. and 8:15 P.M.
Parts of the Sentence Example

1.
How This Book Makes You a Better Writer

The Introductory Essay

Being the author's description of how the basic ideas and exercises of the book fit together, punctuated with snappy remarks and colorful metaphors, opening with a scene from a typical day at work

Terry Johnson comes to work in the morning with a pretty good idea of what she has to do. She has a pocket calendar to keep her schedule. She knows what to do next on her main project. And she is working on a new idea to pitch to her boss.

One reason she has progressed this far in her career is that she plans it, thinking about what has to happen and why. Instead of simply rushing forward with no idea of where she is going, she sets goals. She does not always get exactly what she wants, but she knows how to adjust her goals to changing situations.

When Terry sits down to the keyboard, however, she waits. She waits for the ideas to come, for the words to "flow." After a while she writes down a few sentences. Even though they do not seem right, she finds nothing wrong with the grammar or punctuation. She continues writing, still waiting for that certain click to indicate the writing is "good." At the end of the third run through on her draft, she decides to stop writing, more because she has to get on with it than because she thinks the message is clear.

Terry is uncomfortable because she doesn't know if her memo will have any impact. She wonders if a reader will finish it. She does not want her memo, so important for the completion of her current project, to be treated the way she treats most of the memos sent to her: set them aside for later.

More Joyful Writing

Terry's discomfort is shared by people all over the country, in offices, on assembly lines, at sales desks. Maybe you share it. Or you feel a similar discomfort when you write at work.

Usually the people who worry about their business writing have a good reason. If it is unclear to the writer, it cannot possibly be clear to the reader. Most people, faced with anxiety over their writing, fall back on grammar and punctuation checks. They recall a vague writing tip or two to see if they apply. Sometimes they consult lists of "words not to use" and "words to use." Or they once again read their favorite novelist or magazine writer to see how published writers do it.

These common responses, however, do not solve the problem of Terry's sense of discomfort because they do not focus on the real problem. Writing is not something people do on paper. It is much more. It is observing. It is talking over ideas with others. It is defining yourself. It is expressing. Only one stage of writing gets done at the keyboard or on the memo pad. People who sit down to write without doing the necessary preparation or without knowing what happens after they send off their document will always experience the discomfort Terry feels.

It does not have to be that way.

My Challenge to You: Everything You Think about Writing is Wrong

This book can change the way you write and therefore improve what you can do at work. Survey after survey shows that executives value writing but see little writing of value at work.

Writing is an important part of your job. I don't care what your job is. Today, more than just office writers produce memos and reports. Almost all employees write on the job. A few years ago, a company asked me to provide writing training to people who work on the assembly line of a dental manufacturing plant. Manufacturing hard goods is the last place some people expect to be writing memos. That was once true but it is no more. All employees today write down what they are doing so that managers can stay on top of efficiencies. In addition, in today's complex businesses and public agencies, people make decisions on paper. If you want to suggest an idea, you have to write it down or forget it. Expressing your ideas clearly on paper is necessary so that people in various levels of your company can all evaluate the same thing. If it is not written down, it doesn't exist. It's a rumor.

Work has changed. Writing has changed. That is why I make this challenge to you. Everything you think about writing is wrong. Like Terry, who struggled at the opening of this chapter, maybe you remember a few tips or ideas. Maybe you retain several ideas from grade school. Perhaps you did all right with term papers in college. Maybe you have read other writing books.

I put this statement in your face: prove it! Prove all of it. Begin again by throwing out everything. Examine every assumption, rule, tip, concept or notion you have about writing. In these pages, I will show you a way to write that has worked for hundreds of people who have successfully completed the Write at Work seminars. The ideas and exercises I give you form the basis of how you can start all over again.

Does that mean I have control and you don't? No, just the opposite. The ideas in this book must work for you, or they don't work. Examine each one, understand it, practice it. Then if you find you don't like it, throw it away. Fine with me. Just replace it with a better idea.

You may find that some of the ideas I challenge may work. Okay, keep them if you can prove they work. The single biggest impediment I see for people who want to improve their writing is that they cling to outdated notions about writing. They hold themselves back by feeling that somehow they are not following a rule they learned ten or twenty years ago. Don't do that. Take control. Master the ideas in this book. Add back your original assumptions if you meet my challenge and prove they are worthwhile. At the end you will have rebuilt yourself into an effective writer—your way. One thing that will happen for you as you read this book is that you will see things you are doing right. This book is not about finding what is wrong with people's writing and taking potshots at them. It is about building a better way and feeling comfortable and confident every time you begin to write.

Throughout this book there are exercises for you to do. Many come at the end of chapters. You may believe that you don't need such exercises, and I am sure I cannot change your mind so I won't try. But there are what I call six "core exercises" especially designed to help you identify and master your own individual writing style. These exercises come in the main text of the book and at the end of chapters. I highly recommend that you actually write them out.

The core exercises are:

1. Freewriting
2. The unlocked door
3. Focused Freewriting
4. A return letter to say "no" and
5. Perception
6. Writing a brief report based on a newspaper.

If you take my challenge and complete these exercises, you will improve—no matter who you are or how well you write already.

People More Than Paper

Writing is "people" more than "paper." The path to success for writing dilemmas lies not in learning more rules and tips about language. The solution instead lies in the world around us, its people and problems, its complexities and strains. Writing at work is successfully connecting to this world. So in order to communicate better, Terry must reach out to the people around her rather than isolate herself within the world of language skills. Yes, knowing grammar and punctuation is important. But such language skills are only the tools for communication, not the goals. For writing success, Terry must do what she does in the rest of her work life. She must set goals for each memo, letter or report. And when she finishes, she must check to make sure she has achieved those specific communication and action goals.

Waiting for inspiration to make the words flow will not work. The concept of inspiration comes to us from the ancient Greeks, who identified nine divine Muses who whisper ideas to poets and artists. Unfortunately, the Greeks offer no mention of a Muse for memo writing. For writing at work, they leave us to our own imaginations. That is just as well. We must learn to create our own fate. And for many people today, that fate depends on how well they write. Even with the widespread adoption of computers and the electronic networks that go with them, writing continues to be an essential element for achieving goals at work. In fact, the electronic workplace makes writing skills more important to more workers than ever before.

Maybe you recognized some of the problems Terry faces when writing at work. Her situation is common. If you feel discomfort instead of joy when you write memos, letters and reports, the key to your success is the same as for Terry. Identify your writing process:

Clearly understand the steps you go through to produce a document. Select precise and appropriate communication goals for each writing project. Work until you achieve those goals. And most important of all, once you have achieved the goals you set for yourself, move on to the next task at work without worrying about what you have written. The most enjoyable part of writing does not come from committing words to paper. The pleasant experience we all seek is the fun of knowing you have gotten yourself across to another person, communication fulfilled.

Using This Guidebook

The guidebook in your hands will show you how to identify and set goals for yourself so that writing becomes an enjoyable and effective experience for you at work. You will learn one very effective process for writing any memo, letter or report. This process relies on a format that organizes information on the page in a specific way. The format goes by this abbreviation: LEB123S. This acronym is not a cute, easy-to-remember name. Cute labels for writing formats, besides sounding contrived, make the job seem less demanding than it actually is. Neither is it a magic formula. It is a tool for you. You remain the center of the writing process, not this format. You use it; it does not command you.

The letters of the acronym stand for "Lead," "Explanation," "Background," "First Example," "Second Example," "Third Example," and "Summary." When most people think about writing, they think about words on paper. Successful writers, however, know writing is more than what happens on the page. It is the research before and–for those who write at work–it is the response of readers afterwards that make writing enjoyable and productive.

The heart of this book—the LEB123S format—focuses directly on what happens on the page because that is the best way to communicate to people who want to improve their writing at work. Since that is where you are likely to start thinking about the subject, I will join you at that point and move on from there. The format then becomes a way to discuss the beginning of the writing process and a set of terms for examining the responses of prospective readers.

Once you learn how to organize the language on the page, you will learn ways to determine what content to include in your memos, letters and reports, and why.

But first we solve the most common problem I have seen in more than 15 years of editing and training people how to write. Too many writers shoot without selecting a target. They do not define exactly what success is. Instead, they wait for a vague sense of "rightness" or "flow" after committing words to paper. The sense never comes because it does not exist. Instead—and this is the best news in the guidebook—you are in charge. You determine what success is and you decide what to include in your writing at work. So the first activity is for you to write down what success is. Once you define what you want to achieve (select your target), you will discover a way to hit it. Only then will you experience that good feeling of doing a job well.

Making a Universal Format Your Own

To make this book work for you, begin by writing down "What I like." This book—a mere collection of ink on paper—is nothing until you make it come alive for you. The funny contradiction of **Write Better and Get Ahead at Work** is that the book sets out a single format that each individual writer makes his or her own. Once you decide what you want, the guidebook shows you the format. Original only on the surface, LEB123S is a simple way of stating what you and most readers already know in your hearts. The format is a shorthand way of describing (and remembering) how people in Western Civilization think.

This arrangement of ideas surrounds us in language everyday, in newspapers, at work and in books. You have heard a similar idea before: "Your writing should have a beginning, middle and end." When

I first began teaching writing to people at a community college, I noticed that this strategy did not help them at all. Who could disagree with "beginning, middle, and end"? But what does it mean? What should come first? How do you know which information goes in the middle? How do you know when you have reached the end?

To make the terms of language organization more useful to people who want to improve their work right away, I devised the format to explain exactly what goes into each of the three sections. The format—with variations—applies to any memo, letter or report because it is the fundamental structure of any message, the progression of ideas your reader is expecting to hear. The beginning is a strong lead statement, getting to the point right away with perhaps a bit of explanation to follow. The middle is historical background information and three or so relevant facts to support the lead. The end is a summary, which for writing at work usually means the action resulting from your message.

Where did this format come from? LEB123S comes from the most successful and efficient writing business in the world today: daily newspapers. Compare the writing at most businesses to the writing of a newspaper. In less than 24 hours, a newspaper will produce a story written by one person, edited by two more, reviewed by three or four others and finally printed. The end product is readable, accurate (nearly always), and relevant to the reader now. What happens where you work? Possibly something like this: the boss gives someone a writing assignment; after a day of thinking about it and another day of producing two or three drafts, the writer produces a memo that the boss may or may not like. The final product—even when it is useful for the intended reader—too often feels "wordy" or "boring."

Thinking about Reading

Does this guidebook, then, teach you how to write like a reporter? No. It shows you how people in our society expect to receive information—when they pick up a newspaper or when they pick up your memo. By understanding what readers expect, a successful writer puts those expectations to work for him or her, instead of working against them. "Wordy" and "boring" are probably the two most common terms used to describe work writing in America today. Often used, rarely explained, these criticisms confuse rather than clarify.

"Wordy" usually means the writer does not meet the reader's expectation that a main point will become clear in the first paragraph with background to follow. Too often we make the mistake of chronology by first telling what happened last year, then last week, before finally stating in a memo what people expect: what is happening now. "Boring" is another way of saying the message is not about "me." People the world over value one thing over all else, themselves. I will leave for others the discussion of why immediate self-interest has become the human norm. All I know is that people are first interested in what affects them in their daily lives.

Reader point of view, then, becomes the way to determine what to put into that lead statement. So that becomes the next major exercise of the *Write Better and Get Ahead at Work* guidebook. And off it goes, showing you how to write anything quickly and well with a sense of satisfaction in a job well done.

Much of the *Write Better and Get Ahead at Work* approach challenges common ways of thinking about writing. As you read this book, you will be asked to think differently. One of the major changes will be to move you from "creating writing" to "creating reading." From the beginning, the successful work writer thinks about the reader. In fact, an effective editing technique is to concentrate totally on the reader, organizing information around the reader's life and including only those sentences the reader will want, regardless of how important they may be to the writer.

This guidebook, unlike any other writing manual I have seen, assumes the most important step for writing improvement comes from you, not the author. Throughout each section are exercises so that you can apply new ideas to your workplace immediately. Direct application of writing ideas to what you want to accomplish today is the central purpose of **Write Better and Get Ahead at Work**.

Swing Naturally

While a basic process applies to all writing situations, the guidebook shows you how to create your own personal process and settle on a style of expression that works for you. This book always aims for the target. It provides a method for writing at work that is direct and simple with a minimum of preparation.

Successful writing is like hitting a baseball or dancing. A batter does not swing at the ball by thinking first about flexing his wrists or stepping forward with his front foot. Hitting a baseball is not the combination of many little actions. It is one smooth movement. Breaking down the parts prevents the batter from swinging naturally. The same applies to writing. So the **Write Better and Get Ahead at Work** method aims to make the entire action of writing work as one continuous effort. The techniques offered here serve as "spring training." First, we sharpen the fundamentals then, during the game, we instinctively perform the necessary action smoothly. So too with writing. This book provides the means to practice so that, back at work, when it comes time to write a memo, letter or report, you do it naturally and easily, without worrying about the component parts. When you finish, you feel good about an accomplishment rather than worried about what the reader will think.

For those who do not follow baseball, the same comparison applies to dancing. You take lessons to practice all week, but when Saturday night arrives, you dance smoothly without thinking about where your feet go. Pick either metaphor you prefer. But concentrate on the whole, not the sum of the little parts. If you sit down, well prepared, and express your message by following your own writing process, you will see that the nagging little problems of punctuation or fiddling with this word or that will no longer bother you. Instead, you will swing smoothly and quickly through your writing, confident that you have included the right elements to communicate and get a job done.

Consequently, this book offers exercises on completed work only. Most people motivated enough to improve their writing do not need little grammar exercises or small writing tasks. They want to practice the whole thing. Other than the times when you evaluate some part of your current writing, the exercises are about complete memos and letters or full sections of reports.

After establishing a clear, comprehensive way to write memos, the book builds on this foundation to show you the basics of letters and reports. It explains common types of letters and reports. Many of the most frequent questions in writing courses are about resumes so the book presents a section on writing yours too.

Because everyone can improve his or her writing, following the fundamentals is a presentation on writing excellence. Genius cannot be taught, certainly not by this book. But excellence has a signature. For those who master the basics of writing at work, a later section offers ways to identify, then to achieve excellence. Excellence is even guaranteed at the end of this section (depending on one little condition explained in the text).

Ruling the Rules

Finally we reach what many consider the heart of writing, grammar and punctuation. Unfortunately, this stretch of rules and variations too often becomes the net that entangles writers to the point of paralysis. Usage is important; we need to spell correctly and punctuate sensibly. Yet these rules are the tiny tools of communication, not worth our prime consideration. You most likely mastered most of them by the age of eight or nine. By that time we are speaking the rudiments of our native tongue with no regard to semicolons, split infinitives or passive verbs. It is only when we concentrate on the rules of language—like a beginning dancer trying to control every little movement consciously—that we cause ourselves usage problems.

Nonetheless, the major problems of usage in the workplace today are discussed in the usage section so we can put nagging little problems behind us in order to concentrate on the joy of communicating, the exciting people-to-people aspect of language no matter what we are writing.

Many people who write at work are curious about the public relations trade, especially writing news releases. Needlessly complicated in most places, the news release can be an effective tool for communicating to the general public. The basics shown here include a sample news release and a sample broadcast public service announcement.

You may have noted that I refer to writing at "work" without limiting our scope to the "office." Much writing at work gets done away from a desk by people who do not consider themselves office workers. The **Write Better and Get Ahead at Work** guidebook applies to them as much as it does to the desk bound. This book, however, limits itself to work writing. It helps people write memos, letters and reports. Work writing differs from such writing as short stories, poetry and diary writing in certain ways. Primarily, as the beginning of this chapter explains, we write at work to get something done. Yet the principles you practice here, especially the "Questions to Ask Yourself," will have nothing but beneficial effect on whatever writing you do away from work.

Fast Tips are fun.

Throughout the text, you will see boxes that look like this one. They contain fast tips for getting started, for composing, and for revising your writing. Not exactly real rules, they are little ideas you can use when they are appropriate. Take them in a fun spirit.

About Reference Books

To help you write faster and more clearly, I suggest two reference books, a dictionary and a spell check book. The most serviceable dictionaries is a college the editions because they contain most of the words you will look up yet they do not have the type of reference material you rarely use at work. Spell check books are valuable even for people who already have a spell check function on their computer. Sometimes you want to find a word without

bothering with the computer keystrokes. You've probably seen these books that contain 20,000 words or 30,000 words and resemble a dictionary without definitions. A reference book is a book you can reach from your writing place without having to move. If the dictionary is across the room and shared by others, it's not your reference book. Get you own so you can look up words quickly and get back to real writing. Besides, if you get up to use the common dictionary you are probably just using it as an excuse not to write.

You may have noticed that I am not recommending a thesaurus. These books, with the lists of synonyms, are fine in their own right. But they contribute to problems because people use them incorrectly. I usually see people use a thesaurus by plucking out a word they don't like and substituting a longer word. As we work through this book, we will see that better writing is not about word selection. It is about underlying structure. Changing a word does not change structure. You already know most of the words you need at work. Putting thoughts in order, not selecting fancier words is the key to your improvement. The dictionary and spell checker will serve you just fine.

A Final Word

At this point I am tempted to tell you what I have left out of this guidebook and why. But I won't. ***Write Better and Get Ahead at Work*** is written lean and decisive, including the information you need to achieve your goals as quickly as possible. (Note to editor: I know the words "lean" and "decisive" are adverbs and therefore are supposed to have an "ly" on them. I don't like "ly." It's not lean. I've decided this form does not violate a rule because I am advancing the language here. In 200 years, nobody will be using "ly.") You do not need case studies or histories of letter writing styles. Some information will be most valuable for certain people. For instance, the list of "Questions to Ask Yourself Before Writing the First Word" has helped many people to know when they are ready to start writing so they keep a copy of this page handy. You may want to find a page that helps you with the particular aspect of writing you plan to improve.

I hope that this book helps you become a better, more productive writer so you can get work done the way you want and rise in your profession. ***Write Better and Get Ahead at Work***, tested over the years in classrooms and work sites, addresses many of the problems people are facing in today's workplace. This modest volume is dedicated to stripping away the outmoded thoughts that too often prevent us from communicating with each other happily and productively. The methods of this book more often remove impediments rather than to add to your knowledge. Each of us has the ability to write trapped within us. Freeing our inner potential from anxieties and rules is what expression is all about.

Once you acquire the ability to write by concentrating on meaning and action rather than words and rules, a natural human expression will be clear to your reader who will want to hear what you have to say. Only one way has proven effective to shed the problems and achieve the relaxed effortlessness of a natural writer. Practice.

Your Writing Index

On a separate sheet of paper, respond to each question. Take as much or as little space as you think you need to provide a clear answer.

1. Have you taken writing classes before? If so, which ones? What did you gain from those classes? After taking the classes, what did you decide you wanted to work on?

2. What writing do you do at work–memos, letters or reports? Explain how often you write, why and to whom. What other communications do you have at work (such as meetings, presentations and phone calls)?

3. What is your preferred method of writing–with pen and paper, at a computer keyboard, with a tape recorder or other?

4. What reference books and materials do you use?

5. What books have influenced your idea about writing?

6. How do you describe your communication ability? How do you describe your writing ability?

7. Why is writing at work important to you now and in the future?

8. What do you like best about writing?

9. What do you dislike most about writing?

10. How does writing fit your career goals, and how do you plan to acquire the skills needed to write and communicate at work?

2.
How to Create Reading

Freewriting

Let's begin with a little fun. Rarely do we find anything in this life with a perfectly descriptive name, but one such name is "freewriting." It's one of my favorite writing exercises.

A definition of freewriting packs neatly into one sentence: "Write down whatever you think about for ten minutes straight without stopping." That is it. Nothing more.

Yet so much happens. Freewriting is like the card game bridge. The rules are so exquisitely simple the players have room for unlimited expression. Anything can happen in freewriting.

It is the mirror of literary practices. Try it. You will find you write more and better than you thought possible. You will also, at times, produce garbage. Unstated but necessary to freewriting is constant movement forward. The writer must continue. Must continue. Must continue. Must continue. No room for self-editing, no time for doubt.

Now is a good time to try freewriting for five or 10 minutes.

Once you try it, pause for a moment to capture your experience of the moment. Answer the question "What was it like to freewrite?" Everybody has different experiences, of course. Maybe you experienced what I often feel. At first, I find it hard to write anything. Then something happens—it's like a dam bursting—and I have a torrent of ideas. The task now becomes controlling and channeling these ideas, feelings, images, song tidbits and insights. I like to remember this transition for a particular reason. Sometimes when I sit down to write a memo or letter, I can't think of anything. My mind is as blank as the paper (or screen). Sound familiar? But I don't worry when that happens. I know myself. I have been blank before and I remember that soon a torrent will start. The key for me is to write anything. Then the ideas come. That's why freewriting is helpful for me. I do it regularly.

As you freewrite, you will recognize your own comfortable writing process and will perhaps discover your own way of thinking.

Freewriting is a good way to exercise first thing in the morning. It gets you started when you cannot think of anything to write. It's also a good way to end the day when you only have little time before quitting, not enough time to begin another project. In any event, when the boss walks by while you are freewriting, it looks good.

Most of all, I want you to enjoy freewriting. Writing is fun. Even at work. I enjoy writing, and I want you to enjoy it, too. As we work through this book, we do exercises that are more structured and probably less enjoyable than freewriting. But all writing can be fun—even pounding out the most pressured deadline report at work can be enjoyable. If you get nothing else from this book but a re-connection to the joy of writing, you will have won a lot.

You can find an excellent treatment of freewriting in the book *Writing with Power* by Peter Elbow. Peter has written a new book, along with others, entitled *Nothing Begins with N: New Explorations of Freewriting*.

Defining Terms

In this book, we often use the terms "memo," "letter" and "report." Let's define them before we work on them.

A memo is a one-page document written to someone inside your organization. Because people working for the same company, public agency or non-profit organization already share goals and probably know each other, when they write, they are usually trying to accomplish some specific work goal. A memo is heavy with facts.

When we say "memo," we don't mean "speed memo." Maybe you have seen forms at your company or someplace else that include basic routing information and allow a little space for comment. Speed memos are valuable for certain situations. But we are not talking about speed memos here. When we say memo, we mean a document about a page long, that is, long enough to introduce and carry forward a workable idea.

Letters, however, are between people who do not work for the same organization. So when you write a letter, you cannot assume you share goals and experiences with the reader the way you do when you write a memo. Therefore, a letter often tries to establish a human connection between people, sometimes total strangers. A letter, as we use the word here, is also about a page long.

Fast Tips for starting
1. Complete this sentence: "My reader will want to read my message because...."
2. Say it all in one 2-line sentence.
3. If you are having trouble starting, write down your goal first.
4. Write anything.

A report, I define on the basis of length alone. A report is a written document two pages or longer. The reason for this definition comes from the reader. Think about this from your own experience. When you receive a document two pages or longer, what do you do? If you are like most people, you do not immediately read it. Instead, you devise a strategy for reading it. The strategy usually begins with "I'll read it later." When a person gets around to reading a report, strategy continues. People often do not begin reading a report at the beginning and follow along to the end. They begin by looking for "entry points" such as the list of conclusions or an explanation of methods. So we must write reports with such strategies in mind. Now don't get me in trouble with this definition. If you use a one-page document at work called the "weekly report" or something. Fine. Don't tell your boss that's a "memo," not a "report." I use these terms this way for efficient communication between you and me throughout the book. As always, local rules apply. If your boss calls it a report, it's a report.

Writing for Action

You have no doubt noticed that freewriting is much different from your usual writing at work. For one thing, no one is looking over your shoulder. Freewriting is something just for you. No one approves it or offers criticism.

At work, however, the writing is different. Not only do people see it (and judge us), but also it is directed at a goal. We write because it is necessary. By learning how to write at work and knowing how to do it quickly and well, we increase both our productivity and our enjoyment.

Today, more than ever, people at work must know how to write. Not just people who work at a desk. As computers enter the workplace, information becomes a larger share of each person's daily job. Promotion to a supervisory or managerial position often requires more writing.

People are busier than ever before. With international competition affecting almost every part of society, the push for improved productivity becomes stronger.

We need to be able to write memos, letters and reports quickly, with a sense of accomplishment and confidence. Writing at work successfully means mastering the activity of writing rather than letting it control us.

Even those who gained strong writing skills in school find it necessary to learn the particular composition techniques used in today's workplace. Although experience at writing stories or term papers is valuable in becoming an effective writer at work, these disciplines differ from writing memos, letters and reports in certain important ways.

Writing is also one of those fundamental human activities—such as sports or dancing—that require constant attention to maintain skills. Every person can write better. Even those who have mastered all the skills must try to write faster when they come to work.

Yet mastering the skills of language is not enough. Writing at work is goal oriented—it gets work done. The memo, letter or report is never the end product. At work we do not write for information alone. We write for action.

What I Like

The largest single change most people have to make in order to write effectively is to move from a passive to an active attitude. Instead of trying draft after draft to see if something "sounds right," you must define precisely what you want to accomplish with each writing project.

To arrive at a written product that you like, you first must identify what you like. Think about the messages you have received. Which ones were readable? Which ones struck you just right? Which ones caused you to take the action the reader wanted you to take?

On a piece of paper, list at least five elements you feel make an effective memo, letter or report. (Writing means writing. Running an idea through your mind or "thinking about" five elements is not the same as listing them on paper. Getting into the habit of listing ideas, or outlining or taking notes on paper moves you closer to better writing.)

Reader Point of View

So far, we have discussed leaving out information or including it. Faced with the diverse amount of information coming to anyone's workplace, how do you determine what information is useful for a particular piece of writing and what information is unnecessary? The reader will tell you.

You cannot understand the writing problem as either deciding what to put in or as selecting what to leave out. Both approaches are too narrow. Determining the most effective content means "selecting" among many conclusions, examples, anecdotes, recommendations and facts.

The most effective method of selecting what to include in your writing is to identify what interests the reader. Too often the wordy or clumsy message merely includes content that has no bearing on the reader; it is included only because it interests the writer.

To decide what content will most likely cause the reader to take the action you want, you must adopt the reader's point of view. Taking the reader's point of view is a personal attitude as well as a literary technique.

The following section lists three different versions of a message about recycling. Examine each closely for point of view. See how each subsequent rewrite gains strength and focus by shifting more toward the reader's point of view. (Here is a tip: Writing from the writer's point of view uses the words "I," "we," "us," and "my." Writing from the reader's point of view includes the words "you" and "your.")

"Thank you. We're all refreshed and challenged by your unique point of view. Now, we have many serious matters to discuss today, so I suggest we stick with our agreed-upon agenda."

Writing from the Reader Point of View

Writing from the reader's point of view is an easy suggestion to accept. Everyone agrees with this notion when simply stated. However, when it actually comes time to write a memo, adapting your writing style to the reader is sometimes difficult to do.

Take a look at the three following passages, an original and two rewrites. Then we will discuss them.

Original Version

The company's Recycling Implementation Committee has designed a survey to find out how we recycle and where we can improve. Recycling is one of the major issues we face today. The survey is due back to the committee by the end of the month.

First Rewrite

The Recycling Implementation Committee has decided the best way to recycle at this company is to find out how we recycle already. Once we have responses from all the offices, we can better determine how recycling will help you. We need your answers by the end of the month.

Second Rewrite

To determine the best recycling program for your office, we need to know what you want to do and what works in your office already. This survey from the Recycling Implementation Committee will be used to learn what works now and what you think will work in the future. Let us have your ideas by the end of the month.

The first version, typical of many memos, is about the company's Recycling Implementation Committee. It reads as if it were written by a member of the committee who wants people to know what his or her committee is doing. It adopts a complete writer point of view.

Compare the original to the first rewrite. The first rewrite is about the committee's decision on the best way to recycle. It moves closer to a reader point of view. Instead of being about just the committee, it is about something the committee has done to affect the reader.

So a close analysis will demonstrate point view–reader or writer or somewhere in between. However, there is a faster way to determine point of view, one that will work quickly for you at work. Let's look again at the first two passages to identify the personal words. Those are the words, usually pronouns, which refer specifically to a person.

In the original version, all the personal words are "we," an indication of total writer point of view. The first rewrite includes "we" several times but also contains "you," a reader point of view word.

Now we have a quick way to measure the point of view in any passage of writing. Count the personal words.

Writer point of view words: I, we, us, me, mine, our, and the rest of the pronouns referring to the writer.

Reader point of view words: you, your, yourself. Language has a lot more words for "me" than for "you." Another excellent reader point of view word is the reader's name.

With this method for measuring point of view, let's look at the second rewrite. Count the personal words.

Reader point of view: 5, your, you, your, you, your.

Writer point of view: 2, we, us.

The content of the second rewrite matches the reader point of view of the personal words. It is not about the committee or a committee decision. It is about recycling for the reader. Note also, how the first personal word in the final rewrite is "you."

Having mastered this simple method for determining point of view, take a look at your own work. Count the personal words. Most people have only one or two "you" words in a one-page memo. For most people, the first personal word is an "I" word. There is no rule on what to do. Use the results of your measurement to determine how close you are to the point of view you want to achieve. When you add more "you" words, you'll also see a shift in content, away from your needs and toward the reader's needs. People will like your writing if it is about their needs. Nothing is more important that you. Cole Porter, I think, says it best:

Like the drip, drip, drip of the raindrop, when the summer shower is through
A voice within me keeps repeating you, You, YOU.
Night and day, you are the one,
Only you beneath the moon and under the sun.

Practicing Point of View

Here are some passages written from the *writer* point of view. Rewrite them so that they show the *reader* point of view. (Samples of possible responses are in Appendix I.)

1. So that we can speed up the order, we need all the information listed on the accompanying form.

2. Our services are state of the art. Our response time is the fastest in the business. We have the largest amount of stock available. And we have more locations than any of our competitors.

3. Payroll checks will now come out on the first and the third Friday instead of the second and fourth, beginning next month. Consequently, the series will include one one-week pay period rather than a three-week pay period. Those with individual questions can ask their office managers.

4. I think the project is going well. The other department managers have approved most of the recommendations in your memo. I don't know if you got the schedule at the meeting last month, but the project will probably be completed by the deadline.

From the General to the Specific

From time to time, you will find yourself wrestling with several points to make about one subject. A useful rule to follow is "from the general to the specific." Make the main point first, then back it up with specifics. Here is an example:

"Our department is working too many overtime hours. Last month, the staff totaled 102 overtime hours. That is a 10 percent increase over the previous month."

Helpful with Numbers

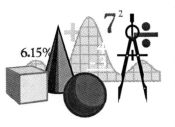

Notice how the writer states the conclusion for the reader. Figures then support the conclusion. While not all specific statements in memos use figures, much information in work writing is conveyed by numbers. When you use numbers, especially if you have a complex array of figures, make a general statement before you introduce them.

A common place for going from the general to the specific is when you are writing an example. In the first sentence of a paragraph, clearly state a conclusion you can support by facts. Then use figures, quotes or eyewitness accounts to illustrate the first sentence. The LEB123S format (Chapter Three) follows the general to specific rule.

The following passages illustrate the general-to-the-specific rule. The general statements are underlined. The first example is simple. Others become more complex.

<u>Our department is the most productive in the company.</u> We were the only department to achieve all of our strategic goals last year.

<u>People who eat a light lunch perform better than those who eat a heavy meal at noon, according to Dr. Angus Craig of the University of Sussex.</u> Dr. Craig, speaking at an American Medical Association sponsored conference, reported that alertness and efficiency reach a low ebb about two hours after one begins eating lunch.

If you write anything—a letter, a memo, a pamphlet, a company brochure, a report—never underestimate the power of anecdotes. If you come upon one in your preliminary research, don't just smile and go on. Take it down carefully; it's valuable stuff—in interest, in reader appeal, in forcefulness, in general all purpose usefulness for written presentation.

—Rudolf Flesch

Practicing general to specific

I'll give you the first, or general, statement, then you fill in the specific. Just like the examples above. You can use the general statement I give you literally, or you can change it a little.

1. General statement: My city is the best in the state.

2. General statement: My city is the worst in the state.

3. General statement: My favorite day of the week is _____. (Fill in the blank.)

4. Now you do a general and a specific.

Using Technical Terms

A technique similar to the general to specific rule applies to using technical terms, sometimes called "jargon." Usually, you do not want to use jargon, the over specialized terms that only a few readers recognize. However, some terms are necessary to include in memos or letters. For instance, for legal or company policy reasons, you may have to refer to a specific program or penalty. Your reader, however, may not be familiar with the terms you must use to make your point.

When you have to use technical terms, try to explain them. Sometimes you may have to say the same thing twice, in two different ways. Such a practice is not unnecessary repetition. Instead, it is writing that achieves two goals; the first goal is compliance with laws or rules requiring the use of certain terms; the second goal is clear communication to a reader who is unfamiliar with the subject. The passage below is an example from an insurance company. Adhering to strict legal guidelines, the writer must inform an injured worker about a particular program. Because disputes over payments may eventually lead to lawsuits, the writer must notify the reader of the exact name of a particular program:

"Because of the length of time you have missed work due to injury, you are required to participate in the vocational rehabilitation program. This mandatory program provides services to help you return to work as quickly as possible."

Note how the writer fulfills legal requirements by using the proper technical term, "vocational rehabilitation program." Then, to ensure communication, in the next sentence, the writer describes the situation in plain words.

About Electronic Mail

People often ask about writing for electronic mail. Is E-mail different from a paper memo? Not really. The same ideas apply. Electronic mail is a tool that accomplishes the goal of communication more efficiently. The same ideas of structure apply: make sure to have a main point, a fact and an action statement. In fact, e-mail only emphasizes one of the characteristics we discuss often in this book: state the main point right away. Sometimes the computer screen shows the email viewer only the first few lines of your message. So your reader makes a judgment quickly on the lead.

*"For the last time, Crawford, our firm is
'warm and fuzzy,' not 'touchy-feely.'"*

The problem that most frequently arises with email is that it allows a
person to do so much so often — maybe too much. You can write forever on a computer screen. It's so simple to go on and on and on
because you no longer have to bother with the complication of typing
and removing typos. Also, it is possible, by electronic mail, to communicate with more people than necessary to accomplish your work goal.

Even with this advance in technology, the eight main questions still
apply. Answer them before you begin to use the keyboard. Stay on your

purpose; keep within your readers' interests. Avoid the all too easy temptation to send the email to everyone in the organization.

Another aspect of electronic communication is speed. With both electronic mail and faxes, people have told me they feel an added sense of urgency to respond. Somehow, they have explained, this seems a game of one-up-manship (I believe this is correctly a male term because it refers to a secondary sex characteristic). Yeah, could be. My suggestion is to go fast. Use the reply function of electronic mail to respond. Fax right back. It gets work out of the way. You don't have to remember to write something and then write it. You just write it. Speed adds value at work.

Exercise

Different Points of View

You work for a major statewide bank as manager of the Remote City branch office, far from the main headquarters in the largest city in the state. The usual method of communication between you and your immediate boss is writing.

As part of the company's *New Business Campaign*, you have devised an employee incentive program to increase deposits and loans at your branch. Your boss, Jim Melman, vice president of branch banking, announced the *New Business Campaign* a couple of months ago. He has asked each branch manager to think up a different, local employee incentive program, which will be part of the larger campaign.

The 11 members of your staff have read about the *New Business Campaign* in the company newsletter. They are waiting for their own local incentive program. You have decided the Remote City program will operate in two parts. Each will last six months. You want to make sure you can make changes in case the original ideas don't work out. At the end of the first six months, you will see how well the program is doing and either continue it or change it for the last six months of the big campaign.

This is how your local program works: Most loans made, a television set; most savings dollars brought in, a microwave oven; second place in each category, a $20 gift certificate for dinner at the Chatterbox Cafe; third place in each category, two tickets to the Remote City High School Homecoming basketball game. All prizes are readily available to you now.

You must write a memo to Melman explaining how your local program fits into his larger campaign. You must write another memo explaining the incentive program to you local staff.

3.
What Readers Want from You

The most frequent question people ask me is, "How do I organize information?" They can collect information and generally determine one or more ideas they want to say. But they are unsure— sometimes to the point of paralysis—of how to put the information down on paper. The most common symptom of this problem is rambling, a document that goes on too long and says too much. Naturally such a memo or letter takes too much time to write.

The solution to this problem lies with the reader. Now that you have absorbed the importance of always taking a reader point of view, let's find out from readers the answer to the question of how to organize. The answer, now tested hundred of times in all types of companies and government agencies, is LEB123S.

The Format for Writing Effective Memos, Letters and Reports

LEB123S allows busy working people to plan and write a document efficiently. You can use this format for messages of any length. Once you practice it a few times, you will understand why it turns writing into a goal-oriented process with a beginning, middle and satisfactory conclusion. If you follow this format, you can be confident you have supplied your reader with information in a way he or she understands.

The name may be new to you, but the format is not. It explains how people think when they read. After years of living in our society, reading books, newspapers and work documents, people build an expectation of how information should be supplied to them. By following this format on paper, you put those expectations to work for you. What follows is this universal format, explained in detail.

1. Lead

This is your main point. It can be a brief, startling statement, a conclusion or a starting point for discussion. The opening is clear and readable in order to make it easier for your busy reader to continue. In a typical one-page memo, the lead is usually one or two sentences long. Get to the point immediately without explanation of the past. State your conclusion or make your recommendation before offering justification. Establish honesty.

The lead has two purposes. They are in this order: Attract the reader's attention. State your main point.

Spend more time writing the lead than any other part of your message. A properly written lead makes the rest of your message easier to organize. Sometimes the writer knows the lead right away; sometimes it takes four or five tries to write enough to discover the best version.

If you are proposing a new idea, state it in the lead so the reader knows what the memo is about.

2. Explanation

The explanation flows naturally from the lead. The lead catches the reader's attention but does not always tell the whole story. An explanation provides more detail, refers to past communication, defines terms used in the lead, or lets the reader know what is coming in the rest of the message. In a typical one-page memo, the explanation is usually the second paragraph.

A typical explanation answers the question "Why?" It might tell why the writer is proposing the new idea now or why the writer is proposing the new idea to this reader.

3. Background

Depending on the situation, a background can be short or long. The distinguishing feature of a background is that it presents past information that is the same today as it was yesterday and will be tomorrow. It sets the lead in context. Background is history. In a continuing discussion of a problem, background remains unchanged. Background helps those new to a situation become as familiar as others who have faced the subject of the lead already. Writers tend to include too much background or to place it too high in the memo, letter or report.

Background is old information so it might refer to past presentations of an idea related to the writer's new idea. The distinguishing feature of background is that it remains unchanged over time. To say we have been working on a particular problem for a month is not background because next month we will have been working on this project for two months. To say we started this project in the summer is background. It's accurate today. It's accurate tomorrow. It's accurate next year.

4. Examples

Each example is a specific incident or reason that justifies the statement in your lead. It supports and proves your lead. Each example in a typical one-page memo is one paragraph. Examples are lean with no opinion. After having read the lead and learned the background, the reader is following your train of thought. Although you are not restricted to three examples, two examples often seem thin, and more than three examples in a typical memo can bore the reader.

The first example supporting a new idea might describe a competitor's success with the idea. The second example might report the results of the idea in another department of your organization. The third example might cite approval from an important manager.

Examples are fact. That means your reader agrees they are accurate. If a reader does not accept your examples as fact, your main point is fatally undercut. The nature of fact is tricky, clearly beyond the scope of a mere writing book focused on practicality. Frequently, the facts your readers accept are numbers.

An advantage of using LEB123S is that you do not have to bother with transitional phrases between examples. List them. Because your reader is now following your train of thought, you can avoid such words as "moreover."

5. Summary

The final paragraph relates to the lead. In longer messages, it can contain a brief summary of the previous points. In almost all cases, the summary includes a clear description of what you want the reader to do: Implement a plan. Talk to you. Review and comment. File. The summary also contains a deadline when applicable. Readers often read only the lead and the final paragraphs so these two segments should contain the basis for your entire message.

A summary might suggest the first step toward putting a new idea into action. In a well-done piece of writing (at work or away), the end connects to the beginning. Such a connection creates a sense of completeness and unity for the reader. Connecting first paragraph with last is a trick of the syndicated columnists you see in your daily newspaper. Read a few of these columnists over the next couple weeks. You will find columns that begin with a particular point, ramble all over the place then finish with a reference to the opening point. Just about the only structural unity to one of these columns is the connection between lead and summary.

For your writing, the connection between lead and summary is the relationship between general and specific. Your lead says, "Doing this is a good idea." Your summary says, "The first step begins Monday." One is a general statement of what we must do. The other is a specific description of what action we must take now.

This format works because it matches reader expectations. When a typical reader picks up a memo, he or she is asking this series of questions: What is this about? Why? How did it get this way? I see what you want, but can you prove it? So now what?

The LEB123S format put these expectations to work for you. It makes it easier for your reader to understand your message. It's faster too. Poor formatting causes the memo to work against the reader's expectations. If your reader is asking, "What is this about?" and you instead give background, you lose the reader right there.

Adapt the format to your needs

After you master the basic format (and you will), you can break away into variations. The straight LEB123S format is a simple, strict approach, like playing the blues. Once you master the fundamentals, you can play jazz, improvisations on the fundamentals. All good jazz musicians are good blues players.

This format adapts to a one-page memo or a ten-page report. You must decide the best way to use the format. In a brief memo, you may choose to eliminate background, compress the lead and explanation into one short paragraph, and reduce the examples to one sentence. In a long report, the lead may expand to a full page with each example turning into a case history one or more pages long.

What remains constant at all times is the central importance of your reader. Now that you understand reader point of view, I never want you to write again. Instead, create reading. Your end product is not ink on paper. It is thoughts in people. The LEB123S format answers the questions a typical reader has at the moment he or she begins to read your memo or letter. Those questions are:

What is this about and is it about me? Why me and why now? What is the context? Can you prove it to me? So what happens now?

Once you master the universal format, you are putting the reader's questions to work for you. Other people are making up a format as they go along, producing (arduously) memos and letters that ignore what the reader is asking. Your writing has the competitive edge.

Let's look at four examples on the following pages.

TO   ■■■■■■■■■■■■■■■■■■■■

FROM   ■■■■■■■■■■■■■■

DATE   ■■■■■■■■■

SUBJECT   ■■■■■■■■■■■■■■■■■■■■■■

Enclosed are the retrospective evaluations on your workers' compensation premium for the July 1, 1985—June 30, 1986, July 1, 1986—June 30, 1987, and July 1, 1987—June 30, 1988, policy years. For the policy year July 1, 1985/86, you can see the retrospective evaluation results in a debit of $26,581 due to an increase in the incurred loss amount. In addition to the retro debit, there is also a Workers' Compensation Department tax debit of $3,747.96, resulting in a net debit to you for this policy year of $30,328.96. Please note that on this second evaluation for the 1985/1986 year you have reached maximum liability. Also attached to the 1985/1986 evaluation is the closure election form (Election for Workers Compensation Insurance Retrospective Rating Plan Agreement). You may, without any additional cost to you, end all premium liability for the 1985/86 policy year by signing the closure election form and return it to me within 30 days in the envelope provided. If you do not elect the closure option on the 1985/1986 year, the premium will be recomputed again in December 1989 and may produce either debit or credit balance based upon any changes in claim costs.

For the policy year July 1, 1986/87, the retrospective evaluation results in a credit adjustment of $11,915.00 due to a decrease in the incurred losses. In addition to the retro credit there is also a Workers Compensation Department tax credit of $1,165.12, resulting in a net credit to you for this policy year of $13,080.12. You may also elect closure for the 1985/86 year, again, ending all premium liability for this policy year. Please be reminded that the election form must be returned to me within the 30 days for the 1985/86 policy year to close. If you do not elect the closure option for the 1985/86 year, it to will be recomputed again in December 1989 and produce either a debit or credit balance.

Also enclosed is the retrospective rating plan evaluation for the July 1, 1987/88 policy year. This is the first evaluation for this policy year. As noted, the plan resulted in a credit of $13,258.00 plus a Workers Compensation Department tax credit of $1,510.34 resulting in a net credit of $14,768.34.

Attached with these retro evaluations you will find a statement of account. The bottom line adjustment for the three policy years (1985/86, 1986/87, 1987/88) results in a retro debit of $2,480.50. ■■■■■ must receive payment by April 28, 1989, to avoid any interest charge. Interest will accrue at a rate of 1% month if the debit is not received by this date.

If you have any questions or I may be of any further assistance, please do not hesitate to call me at ■■■■■■■■.

A Look at the First Example

Note the numbers in the first paragraph. I see many memos that begin this way. A reader does it in order to get right to the point, the facts and figures of the matter. But the facts and figures are never the point; they support the point. The point revolves around the needs of the reader, which are nowhere acknowledged.

With the new format in mind, how would you characterize the first paragraph? It is an example, actually a series of examples. The reader cannot absorb these figures because he or she has no way of knowing what they are for. It is like loading up a shopper with 30 items from the grocery store shelves. No one can hold that much stuff. First they need a shopping cart. The shopping cart that helps the reader hold all these facts and figures is a lead. State the main point first then support it.

So much for the way it begins. What about the end? The summary is the last two paragraphs. Both are action items, just as they should be. Generally, I like the end. However, it uses a common message: call me if you have questions.

Too many writers allow the "question message" to serve as the action summary. No good. The point of your job is not to get people to ask questions. It is to sell something, or deliver it, or to accomplish some other kind of work. Effective writing advances that work. The action summary must be about what you want to accomplish. The second to the last paragraph of this example does that.

So it's okay to include the question message. But it not sufficient to rely on it for your action summary. If you want to use the question message because it shows politeness and respect for the reader, do so before the specific action summary. In this example, I suggest reversing the order of the last two paragraphs.

Finally, you see this example is a letter, not a memo. Usually the LEB123S format is used for memos. In a later chapter we cover a format for letters. However, the format is universal. It is usually reserved for memos because it is these internal documents, heavy with information, that do the most work. This example is a fact-heavy letter. It is a type of letter sent so routinely by the writers at this company that it functions as a memo.

Now that we have a sense of what a lead is and how it works with the action statement, we can look at how to use the format to understand how all the parts of a memo fit together.

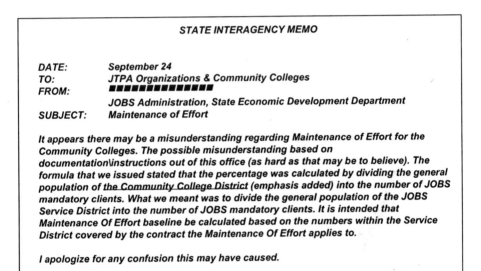

> **STATE INTERAGENCY MEMO**
>
> **DATE:** September 24
> **TO:** JTPA Organizations & Community Colleges
> **FROM:** ▬▬▬▬▬▬▬▬▬▬▬▬▬
> JOBS Administration, State Economic Development Department
> **SUBJECT:** Maintenance of Effort
>
> It appears there may be a misunderstanding regarding Maintenance of Effort for the Community Colleges. The possible misunderstanding based on documentation\instructions out of this office (as hard as that may be to believe). The formula that we issued stated that the percentage was calculated by dividing the general population of the Community College District (emphasis added) into the number of JOBS mandatory clients. What we meant was to divide the general population of the JOBS Service District into the number of JOBS mandatory clients. It is intended that Maintenance Of Effort baseline be calculated based on the numbers within the Service District covered by the contract the Maintenance Of Effort applies to.
>
> I apologize for any confusion this may have caused.

A Look at the Second Example

Here's what we all dread. A local newspaper found one of this poor guy's memos and splashed it all over in order to make fun of him. (After finishing this book, you can be confident this will never happen to you.) Except for eliminating the name, the memo here is exactly as it was sent out and printed in Willamette Week newspaper as the *Memo of the Week*. I have left out the jokes that newspaper told at the writer's expense.

Most people are stunned when they see this memo. You may be surprised to hear that my impression of this memo is that it is not so bad. You may see several points you want to raise about sentence construction or other matters of usage, but let's focus only on the organization of ideas only in order to see how the format can work. I think of this memo as being crushed by some kind of literary compactor. Except for half a line at the end, it is all one paragraph.

If we unravel it a bit, we can see it follows the format. The first sentence is a lead. The second is background. The next two sentences, the old formula and the new one, are examples. The final sentence in the big paragraph, although it is hard to understand in passive voice, is an action summary.

So the format gives a way to break this block of type into paragraphs. Next I suggest a small paragraph as example one, the old, incorrect formula. Then the next paragraph needs to be long enough to explain the correct formula in detail and to emphasize its importance.

What about the final line? Again, the format helps us solve a problem. First, we identify what the line is. Since it answers the question of why I am writing, it is explanation. This apology works best if it follows the lead so it moves to right behind the first sentence.

Applying the format to this paragraph shows us more than just how to use the new skill to improve our writing. This example demonstrates that the format comes naturally to people. The writer of this memo has never heard of LEB123S, yet his work, in an overly compact, impersonal way, follows the format.

The next example shows how the format stretches to provide an effective structure for longer works.

TO:	▪▪▪▪▪▪▪▪▪▪▪▪▪
FROM:	▪▪▪▪▪▪▪▪▪▪
SUBJECT:	Employee Spot Awards
DATE:	October 16, ▪▪▪▪

The spot award program might possibly be eliminated from our division. Any future spot awards that our top-level managers want to give their employee's will not have the capability of doing so, if we don't have some stiffer guidelines.

After reviewing the spot award report of gifts, a red light came on for me that our top-level managers have been giving the "great job" gifts to any employee, which means, employees from other divisions. According to the guideline policy for giving these awards, it is specified that only a top-level manager may give their employee(s) an on the spot award. After reviewing the report, 16 out of 23 top-level managers have been giving the spot awards to any employee outside of our division.

My request to you is that you support my idea about updating the division guidelines for our spot award program, create an addendum to the previous policy and make the necessary changes, so in the future the spot award program will not be eliminated from our division from misuse. The report also indicated that our division is allocated $5,000.00 a year for spot award gifts and as of today we have spent $4,950.00. As you know the spot awards are given to an outstanding employee who has been recognized for their effort, team spirit, hard working, and going the extra mile. The additional individuals who have been accomplishing those skills cannot be recognized, because our division is out of money, due to the fact that it was spent on employees outside of our division.

Please review the attached spot award report and when we meet on Monday, October 18 for our weekly staff meeting we can discuss the issue and make some needed changes. I feel confident that you will support my enthusiasm about this subject a long with helping me make the necessary changes to keep our spot award program within our division.

A Look at the Third Example

Here's a problem I see all too often. A buried lead obscures an important idea. This memo starts with the problem – not the solution. The writer wants to improve and update the Spot Awards Program. We don't really learn that until the third paragraph ("My request to you...")

People don't want to read about problems. In most cases, they are all too familiar with the problem at hand. They are excited, however, when they can read about solutions. The writer reports her enthusiasm toward the end of the memo. If she focuses on the solution from the beginning, here enthusiasm draws the reader into the memo.

By putting the problem in the lead, this writer than uses examples to prove the nature of the *problem*. Such information is better handled in condensed form as background. Better to lead with the solution as your main idea and follow with examples that support the requested improvement.

Burying the lead is a small enough problem in a memo. It gets really out of hand with a report, a document of more than two pages. Too often people spend time and effort researching a problem at work. Then they pile past problems into the front of a long document, leaving the new and exciting information about proposed solutions at the end— long after the reader has given up.

TO: Eileen Dent, Secretarial Supervisor

FROM: Phyllis Misenar, Word Processor

SUBJECT: Word Processing Instructions for New Employees

DATE: April 29, 1991

Your staff's work will be more efficient if new employees are given instructions about Bureau of Traffic Management word processing procedures.

procedures you have outlined.

Several years ago the attached instruction packet was handed out to all new employees whose job included generating documents on the computer. This procedure has gradually fallen into disuse.

Besides guiding the new employee to the section regarding preparing word processing documents in our Policy and Procedure Manual, some of the ways these instructions are helpful are:

- such as using indents correctly and putting two spaces after the end of sentences within a paragraph;

- indicating attachments and copies, sending mass mailings and proofreading; and

- Gives other information regarding using conference rooms, the reception area and the sign-in sheet.

new employees.

Attachment

A Look at the Fourth Example

Now, you decide what works and what doesn't. Look beyond the surface of the sentences to see the internal structure. What seemed seamless at first to you now becomes a blend of working parts.

You Are in Charge: Variations on a Format

For this process to work productively for you, you need to understand an important point. You are in charge. The LEB123S format (or any other way of going about writing) can only work if you control it rather than the other way around. Using a format is much like communicating in a language. When you sit down at work, you are spared the difficulty of deciding which language to use today. Of course, you use English. Yet this "limitation" does not restrict your creativity. The same with a format. It is a tool you use to achieve what you want; not a straight jacket to prevent you from thinking.

The beauty of this format is that it applies to nearly all writing at work. When you have a writing job to do, you sit down at the beginning with the confidence that you will produce a strong lead to grab the reader's attention, fill in the background later and end with an action statement. The value of this format is that you can control it, creating variations—long, short and in between—to solve the specific problem at hand.

Short variation on standard format

We have seen how the format applies to a typical one-page memo. Sometimes you need to get your point across in a few lines. Sometimes you have to write a report. We will discuss reports later on. Right now, let's look at using a format in shorter notes. An example follows:

Direct deposit of your payroll check into a bank account is now available. If you want to have this service beginning with the first check after the 15th of next month, you need to sign up in personnel. The payroll clerk now has a form for you to fill out.

This three-sentence note—perhaps a "stuffer" in a pay envelope—follows the LEB123S format. The first sentence is the lead. Even though it reaches all employees, it is addressed to one individual. The beginning reports what is happening to the reader now. No explanation is necessary. Background is not included probably because this service was announced earlier and described in detail at that time, perhaps in the employee newsletter.

The second sentence includes two facts that support the opening statement: available on the 15th of next month and requires a sign up in personnel.

The third sentence is an action summary: go to the payroll clerk to fill out a form.

An evaluation of this note shows that it successfully achieves the purpose of telling employees that the direct deposit service is now available. Once people sign up with the payroll clerk, we know the communication found its intended readers, and the note is successful. Likewise, if no one signs up, we have reason to believe something is wrong. Maybe the note was not delivered correctly.

So the principles of writing for action apply even to small writing tasks. This note was made short by eliminating the least important information. An equally short note that includes background but not a clear action statement will not succeed. What matters is that you, the writer, decide what goes in (two factual examples) and what is unnecessary for this specific writing job (no explanation, no background). You are in charge, not the process.

Many variations are possible. The three examples can all be in one sentence. Or you can include seven examples if each one provides necessary support for your lead. Maybe background is important,

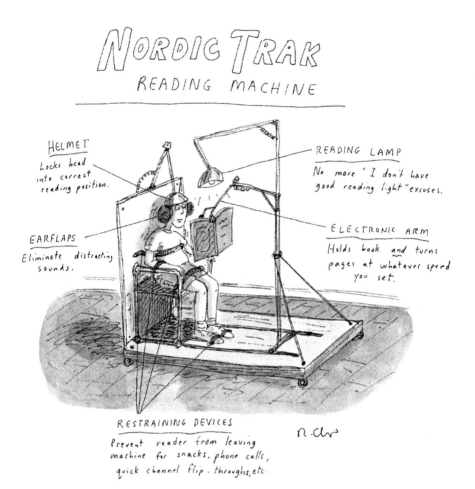

NORDIC TRAK
READING MACHINE

HELMET
Locks head into correct reading position.

EARFLAPS
Eliminate distracting sounds.

READING LAMP
No more "I don't have good reading light" excuses.

ELECTRONIC ARM
Holds book and turns pages at whatever speed you set.

RESTRAINING DEVICES
Prevent reader from leaving machine for snacks, phone calls, quick channel flip-throughs, etc.

especially if you are writing about an old problem and you expect a new person to read a particular memo.

Your lead may state a conclusion so unusual you may have to include a lengthy explanation stating why now, why this reader, or more, and only one fact is relevant. Controlled, informed decision making is what you need.

For reports, the introductory lead may be a page long, stating the name of the person who commissioned the report, the time period of the research and the way the reader should use the report. An example may be a case study running several pages long. For report writers, research is rarely the problem. They get stuck when they have so much information they do not know how to present it coherently.

If that happens for you, use the format to find a "lead"; identify all historical information to compile into "background"; separate each incident or case study into different "examples"; and when you have done that, your summary will be clear to you. A format is most valuable when the writer faces a large writing job.

My Writing Process

It is an ugly word. But it is the right word, "process." Writing at work cannot be haphazard or disorganized. Like any other project at work, it must be clearly defined, set within the context of your organization and focused on a goal.

Such an emphasis on process—with its connotations of bad cheese or auto assembly lines—may seem to take the fun out of writing. Not at all. Writing combines both routine techniques and individual expression to create a final product. Lost in the struggle with technique—punctuation, format, opening sentences—many people never find their way to the joy of personal expression. Mastering such common elements of language as punctuation and grammar, although necessary, will not make you an effective writer. Only by taming the techniques of language into a process that you control can you free yourself to add the "personal touch" that stamps your signature to what you write.

What does "process" mean? It means everything about the activity of writing from the moment an idea occurs to you until the time somebody reads what you have produced. It happens on paper and in the rest of your life.

Once most writers begin to concentrate on creating a consistent writing process focused on an organized, readable structure, they realize they feel comfortable with one of two general approaches. Many writers like to write the lead paragraph over and over until they get it just right. Once they know how to grab the reader's attention with a precise message, they can go on to include background and supporting examples. As a result of my years in journalism, this is the approach I prefer.

Other writers prefer to write in a let-it-flow fashion. By writing, they are actually thinking through the situation. Such a writer may produce three or four paragraphs before realizing the actual message. It is at this point that understanding your personal process is most useful. Too many writers, finding that their message has changed as they write, feel they have hit a frustrating block. They cannot see how to organize their work in a clear, coherent fashion. LEB123S format, by labeling different types of paragraphs according to their organizational roles, helps them decide what to do next.

Vertical Approach

The vertical approach is more common. See if this situation feels familiar. You write for a while, about four or five paragraphs. You like the last paragraph you write, figuring it neatly captures what you want to get across. Yet, as you look back at the other paragraphs you wrote, you see no clear connection to the last one. Nor is it clear what you want to write next. I call this the vertical method. The only organizational structure is that one paragraph follows another down the page.

This is one of the most common experiences writers have at work. The next step is crucial to success. Too often people get mad at themselves at this point and begin to feel anxiety about writing. By using the writing tools we have mastered so far, we can see that this common point in the writing process can change from frustration to success.

We know from the format that what the writer has produced in that last paragraph is a lead. It moves to the front. The first couple of paragraphs are warming up to the point, just the way the reader did in the fourth example we looked, the newspaper opinion piece. Sometimes, in this situation, these warm ups are effective background. Or they may contain a factual example that supports the lead.

After identifying the paragraphs as elements of LEB123S, the writer puts them in proper order. Adding an action paragraph usually completes the memo. There. We're done. Time not for anxiety but for a coffee break.

Other strategies are useful when you reach this point, finding your lead after about four or five paragraphs. Sometimes you can cut out the first few paragraphs entirely. People hesitate to cut because they think they are wasting something. But remember you are not writing anymore. You are creating reading. Cutting is sometimes the best way to strengthen a memo (I'm sure you've seen several examples).

Horizontal Approach

Another common method for putting ideas down on paper (or up on a computer screen) is writing the lead over and over until you get it right. That's what I do. It's a common habit of reporters and ex-reporters.

First, I write worthless crap. Then mediocre junk. The next try is adequate. Finally, I distill my vague impulse of an idea into words that attract my reader and get the main point across. Since I am writing the same thing over and over, I think of the movement as lateral so I call this the horizontal method.

Sometimes, because in my research stage I know what my final structure will be, I can write a clear lead the first time. Usually, that's because I have to. On occasion, I am called upon to write a news release. It is the nature of such a task to have to move quickly. That's why a client turns to someone like me—not because I know his or her business so well, but because I can write about it fast.

Once I went to work for an advertising agency to do public relations for them. Obviously, I thought, they hired me away from my previous job because of my talent, expertise and general charm in dealing with others. The first day on the job I find out the real reason. The hiring process had lasted for a couple of months over conversations with several people. But it was only when I was actually working for them that they told me the first thing I had to do. The agency had promised to write and place a major article in a prestigious professional publication. They were too ashamed to admit that anxiety over writing a long piece had paralyzed them.

That first day someone showed me the total of their labor over the past three months, one page of disorganized notes. This unimpressive output had been accumulated at the cost of several thousand dollars to the client for meetings and "writing" that I assumed was the single page of notes.

Fast Tips for starting
5. Write a "bad" sentence you know you won't have to use.
6. Freewrite and throw it away.
7. Compile all your research within arm's reach.

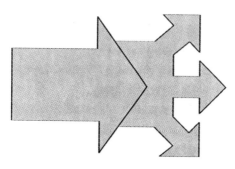

The deadline was on them. They needed a magazine article now. I said okay. At that moment I knew exactly how I would structure the article. After a clever, tough, reader-oriented main point that left some unanswered questions, the article would explain professional terms before setting the main point in the background context of trends in the industry and moving on to several examples concerning the client and finishing with a bang that makes sure to answer all the questions raised at first. Does that structure sound familiar to you?

What was clear from the "notes" was the absence of a main point. I interviewed the client for the sole purpose of finding one. Once I did, I wrote about a dozen versions of the lead, re-organized the notes into something readable, visited the library for professional background and slapped on an ending that consisted of a joke that I thought of while I was writing something else where it didn't fit. The client threw a party when the article was published in the leading professional magazine for the industry.

That's what I want you to do. Face any writing situation with the confidence that you have a way to structure the ideas and you know your writing process.

Which of these two general approaches appeals more to you? Do you write a lead over and over until it is just what you want to say? Or do you write one paragraph after another until you see the point you want to make? You won't improve your writing until you determine your approach. While the horizontal and vertical methods are the most common, they are not the only ones.

Other Approaches for Capturing Your Words on Paper

People develop a variety of ways to put ideas on paper. This list shows all the major ones I can find. Do any work for you?

- Write out the examples first (useful in long reports)
- List key points or key words
- State the action goal
- Outline with or without Roman numerals
- Draw "idea maps" with lines connecting related concepts
- Answer the relevant questions on paper
- Freewrite until a good idea comes.

Earlier, we mentioned that "process" is not restricted to words on paper; instead, the term covers the whole way an individual writes. That includes idiosyncrasies such as always having a cup of coffee at hand or preferring to write at a certain time of day. You have your preferences, too. Know them.

Listed below are some elements of what could be your writing process. They help you start writing. They are not listed in order of importance or any other order. Some will apply to you; some will not. They are just a few examples of the many aspects of life that go into defining a person's writing process. Identify the elements of your own process.

___ Collecting thoughts on paper

___ Outlining

___ Writing a lead over and over until it is right

___ Reading out loud

___ Answering key questions

___ Writing down the overall goal

___ Listing my readers

___ Waiting for the last minute to put pressure to work for me

___ Scheduling enough time so I can write something; let it sit for a while and return to it with a fresh eye.

___ Writing a rough draft first

___ Composing into a tape recorder.

If you never decide your own process, you will forever be caught in a frustrating twilight zone of revisions, never sure of which way to turn next. Find out which general approach works best for you, identify the elements of a process that help you and practice them.

Getting Used to the Format

1. TO LABEL IS TO MASTER

Find five memos at work. Label each paragraph with the descriptions from the format: lead, explanation, background, example or action summary. If the paragraphs are in an ineffective order, arrange them better. You are likely to find at least one memo with no lead at all, like the first example in this chapter. Write one.

2. YOUR TURN

Find five memos or letters you have already written. Do to yourself what you did to other people in exercise one.

3. TRY THE HORIZONTAL APPROACH

The next time you write a memo or a letter containing much factual information, write the lead first. Don't go on until you are satisfied with your lead paragraph. In a typical one-page memo or letter, the lead runs four to seven typewritten lines.

4.
Deciding What to Say

Now that you know how to organize information in a memo, from lead to summary, you face the question of what to say. Most people at work struggle with one of two approaches to this problem. Either you have too much information to contain on a page, or you do not have a clear idea of what to include.

If you have enough information—maybe you have been doing research and talking to others for a while—but you do not know what to include, you can use the format by plugging information into the various parts. Some people will see they are strong on examples because they have many specific facts (engineers are good at knowing the exact facts of a message). Some people will see they have much background information so they will be able to put the message into proper context. Either way, you can fill in what you have, then add a lead or summary or whatever is missing. If you fill all the parts of the LEB123S format, you know you have written a comprehensible document that others can follow. The format can also help you edit. Once you have the information necessary to fulfill the format, you can probably stop writing. Usually, this means cutting down some of your background or using three examples instead of six. Remember, you are trying to get a specific action accomplished, not listing everything you know about a subject.

The process of filling in a few parts will sometimes stimulate a writer to complete a missing part, often the lead. How does this suggestion of plugging in the parts of the format compare with the individual writing process you worked out earlier? Do you want to make adjustments to your personal approach?

If you have the opposite problem—not enough information—the format tells you what to look for. Start with any part of the format you feel comfortable with. Look for a lead or look for some facts to build examples. Maybe you know what action you want the reader to take. If you have enough information to do part of it, good. Then maybe you still have some research to do. Save what you have done and get up from the keyboard to find the information you need to complete your memo, letter or report. Maybe at this point you need to talk to somebody else about the subject.

No matter what, when you feel stuck, do not sit at the keyboard hoping to think up something to say. Such a passive approach never accomplishes the goal. Once you identify how you work, you may see it is part of your process to write a little bit to clarify your intent before doing further research to get the information that will lead your reader to act. So instead of getting frustrated when you reach an impasse, simply recognize such a situation as a constructive stage of your own process.

Shared Experience is the Basis of all Communication

Your reader tells you what to write. The possibilities of what to say in any one situation are uncountable. But your memo, letter or report will only be effective as long as it addresses your reader's needs.

Remember the three versions of the passage about recycling we looked at in the section on Point of View? In the original version, the writer proudly notes his or her committee designed a survey, a fact that is important to the writer's job and self esteem, yet meaningless to the reader. In the first rewrite, the writer mentions recycling in this company, an activity that at least affects the reader directly. Finally, in the second rewrite, the writer concentrates on what is most likely to interest the reader, improved recycling in the reader's office. The Recycling Implementation Committee, the center of attention in the first version, is rewritten into a lesser role in the final rewrite.

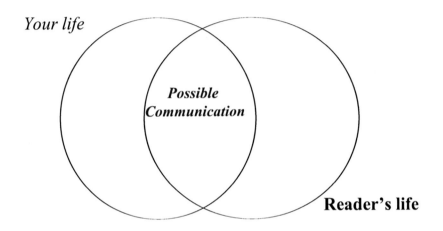

The lesson applies to all aspects of writing, from researching to proofing. The accompanying simple diagram illustrates the writing situation. Your writing comes only from the circle that represents the experiences of your own life, naturally. The reader's understanding, however, depends on the circle representing his or her life (just as naturally). Consequently, the basis of communication is your shared experience. Don't write about the part of the circle only you know. You can't write about the part of the reader's circle that you don't know. Write about the overlapping wedge in the middle. Ask yourself not, "What is my subject?" Ask, "What do I share in common with my reader within this subject?" The beginner writes about the himself or herself. The apprentice writes about the subject. The professional writes about the reader.

Questions to Ask Yourself before Writing the First Word

To make it easier for you to assume the reader's point of view, the following eight questions will help you identify and remember what your reader wants in each writing situation. You can use the questions in various ways. They help you get started when you are not sure what to say. They offer a way to rethink a problem when you get stuck. And when you have finished writing your memo, letter or report, these questions serve as check points to ensure you have included all the necessary information.

The questions cut through the clutter and extraneous information crowding any writer's mind. When composing a particular document aimed at accomplishing a goal at work, do not concern yourself with the whole of the reader's point of view. Instead, focus on the part of the reader's world that overlaps yours.

The same need for direct, immediate relevance applies to the writer. While you may be writing for five important reasons, perhaps only one of those reasons will have relevance to the reader. So where your world touches the reader's world is the region of communication. The following eight questions help you see any writing situation from the point of view of the reader

The Eight Questions

1. What is my purpose? And should my message be written?
2. Who is reading this?
3. What are my readers interested in?
4. How much do they know already?
5. Will something besides my written message—such as a product sample or photograph—help them to understand or to act?
6. What other communication (memo, meeting, conversation) in the past or the future is involved?
7. What specific action do I want my reader to take or expect me to take once he or she has read the message?
8. Is there a deadline? If so, when?*

* "As soon as possible" is not a deadline. A deadline happens at a certain time such as noon on Friday of next week.

To practice using these questions, a sample writing exercise follows on the next page. "Unlocked Stockroom at Natural Manufacturing," a story problem, requires you to write a memo to your staff. Read the story problem and answer the eight questions for this situation.

Unlocked stockroom at
Natural Manufacturing
An exercise

Last night, for the second time in as many months, the door to your stockroom was found wide open by a security guard in the early morning. Lately, the stock supply expenditures have been high for your company.

Your firm, Natural Manufacturing, Inc., occupies three floors in the building. You are in the marketing department with seven staff people, including two support staff. The only other occupant on the floor is the finance department of your company. Marketing and finance are the only two offices using the supply room on this floor. Besides the usual assortment of paper and pencils, the stockroom also holds spare electronic typewriters, tape cassettes, photographic equipment and other valuable supplies.

You are the manager of the marketing department. Lewis Cannon, the executive vice president, who is your immediate boss, has asked you to take care of this problem immediately. Marketing uses many more supplies than finance, and your staff tends to keep odd hours, often working past 5 p.m. Cannon has not been happy with the company-wide high cost of supplies for some time. Now he is very displeased that your stockroom has been found unlocked again. He said he might remove the stockroom from your floor, requiring everyone on that floor to have to request supplies from the office manager of the floor above yours. The manager of the finance department, B. N. Counter, who also reports directly to the executive vice president, has agreed that you can communicate directly with her employees; she supports whatever decision you make.

You need to write a memo to the employees involved.

Use the English Language, or CC Ya' Later

Soon you will identify how you write and comfortably write dozens of memos easily and naturally using the standards established by the LEB123S format. Your writing will be simple and clear. It will be your personality on paper.

One of the drawbacks of not writing with such professional naturalness is relying on foreign phrases. They cause more confusion than anything else. People understandably resort to such phrases because they have seen them for years and assume they give their writing a tone of professionalism. They don't. Professionalism, as we have seen, comes from taking reader point of view and using an effective structure.

Let's have some fun with this one. Listed here are foreign phrases to avoid. People use them all. The more obscure ones are explained in parentheses. Imagine how pretentious they sound, and laugh.

ad hoc
as per
bon mot (witty remark)
carpe diem (write "act quickly")
cause celebre
cc (write "copies")
coup d'état
de rigueur (necessary)
e.g. (for example)
esprit de corps (team spirit)
etc.
et al. (and more)
ex post facto (after the deed is done)
fait accompli (done)
i.e.

in camera (secretly)
in situ (the original situation)
inter alia (among others)
in toto (totally)
ipso facto (facts prove)
magnum opus (major undertaking)
modus operandi (only if you are a detective)
nota bene
par exemple (for example)
per capita
per diem
per se
prima facie (on the face of it)
pro forma (routinely)
pro rata (proportionally)
quid pro quo (this for that)
RSVP
re
sic (as in the original)
semper ubi sub ubi (always wear underwear)
sotto voce (a whisper loud enough to hear)
status quo
sui generis (one of its own)
tempus fugit
terra incognita (unknown)
tour de force (done with strength)
via (by way of)
vis-a-vis (face to face)
vox populi (popular opinion)

Where Are We Now? A Brief Review

You best understand writing at work, like other types of writing, as a unified act of creativity. People often go wrong by thinking of writing as a compilation of words or a mere succession of ideas. Writing, like hitting a baseball or dancing, is a smooth movement, not a collection of smaller pieces stuck together.

Distinguishing writing at work from other forms of writing is its goal orientation. We write memos, letters and reports to get something done, either an immediate action or a long-term goal for the entire organization. Like other activities at work, writing must be planned toward a defined goal. Waiting for the right words or looking for a sense of flow will achieve no goal.

Changing your word selection rarely improves writing. To keep readers on track, recognize their point of view. Then organize your work with a simple, consistent, easy-to-recognize underlying structure. Find your most comfortable methods for researching and organizing your thoughts. Practice those methods over and over so you become better each time.

Because readers—customers, fellow employees, managers—are busy, they want to read messages that follow an identifiable structure. The most effective construction organizes the points this way:

- *Lead* attracts the reader's attention and says the main point.

- *Explanation* follows naturally from the lead to answer questions arising immediately such as "why write now?"

- *Background* sets the new idea in context with historical information.

- *Examples* supply factual support to the lead. They can be single numbers or long case histories.

- *Summary* explains the action the reader is expected to take or the writer will take. While the lead will talk about a general course of action, the summary pinpoints exact steps to be taken such as discussing a problem at the next staff meeting.

While a typical page-long memo may follow the format exactly, with a section covering each element of LEB123S, variations are often necessary. Background or explanation can be eliminated. More or fewer than three examples may be needed to motivate the reader to act. The decision to cut or lengthen belongs to each writer, who uses the format as a tool rather than following it as a command.

To organize writing in a readable format efficiently, identify and practice an individual writing process. This process includes everything the writer does from the moment a decision is made to write to the time a reader receives the memo, letter or report. Individual processes vary widely. Experimentation is usually necessary to find the best set of elements to include in your process.

Once you are comfortable with a process for producing an organized message on paper, select the proper content for the lead, explanation, background, examples and summary. In the middle of a complex world, the best way to determine effective content is to learn what matters to the reader and adopt a reader point of view. If you know your process and you understand the reader, and you are still stuck, the most likely problem is lack of research. Get up from your writing place and gather more information.

Fast Tips for starting
8. Answer the 8 questions.
9. Write your action statement.
10. Write three complimentary statements about your reader.

An effective aid to mapping out the content of any message is to answer the eight questions:

- What is my purpose?
- Who is reading this?
- What are the readers interested in? How much do they know already?
- Can I send along an item to make my message easier to understand?
- What other communication is involved?
- What specific action do I want to take place as a result of reading this memo, letter or report?
- What is the deadline for this specific action?

Writing Practice Memos

1. CHANGES

Recommend a change to your boss. Find any practice, procedure or aspect of work you think should be changed. Write a one-page memo about it. You can suggest a major overhaul of policy or a change in the way the furniture is arranged. Review an old practice or comment on a new one. Anything about change.

2. BOOKS ON WORK

Explain the value of a work-oriented book (even this one) to your boss. Is it valuable to others in the office? Include facts to support your general supposition. Possible action includes recommending the boss read it or not, or suggesting some other use in the office.

3. ACCOMPLISHMENTS

What have you done for me or anyone else lately, like today? Pick a day between now and next week. Write a memo to your boss about what you have *accomplished*. Don't simply list what you did and leave it at that. Make a judgment; reach a conclusion. Most work days are a succession of only marginally connected events. Take this diverse list of incidents and shape it into a memo. Organize your memo in terms of what you do for the entire organization. Remember your reader.

Variations: Write to your job placement counselor, write to a teacher.

4. BINDER BIND

You work in the accounting office of Natural Manufacturing Company. You just paid a bill for manila binders for your department. The bill, for one month's worth of binders, is $1,437.58. Your company must keep track of many customers, retail outlets, products and distribution areas. That's why you use so many binders.

You pay so much because you use the best, most expensive binders available. They work great. Binders in each office are identical and they serve the various needs of each department. They come in 25 color codes so they are easy to separate and use. The binders your company uses are here as a result of a consultant's recommendation seven years ago.

However, you know the beautiful binders are "overkill." A less expensive binder will do a good job for less money although no other binder is as good as the ones you use. As far as you know, no one has thought about saving money on binders.

Two brands of binders especially are attractive to you. "Preti-Good Binders" cost $74 per carton and come in five color codes. They are nearly as sturdy as "Fine Binders," the brand you use now, which cost $100 per carton (same number). "Good 'Nuf" Brand binders are $50 per carton (same number) with no color coding included. They are thinner than the other two.

Write a memo to your boss in accounting, B.N. Counter, suggesting a change.

5. AND NOW THIS IMPORTANT WORD

Your boss in word processing has asked you to draft a memo over her signature. She is the supervisor of word processing, Lotta Pages. You and one other person do the entire word processing for the company.

The policy has always been that memos and letters up to two pages long will have a turnaround time of no more than two hours from the time a draft is submitted to the time a finished product is ready for review. The problem is that most people bring their work to you (dictating machine tapes and hand drafts) at around 3 p.m. While the whole rest of the day may be slow, your staff is consistently overwhelmed late in the day, causing too much overtime.

Lotta Pages' boss has authorized her to change the policy to say the turnaround in the morning will remain two hours, but there will be no turnaround guarantee in the afternoon.

This strikes you as an appropriate time to announce a new function in word processing that few people are using. Word processing is accessible on the central computer. Staff can now keyboard in a memo or letter and notify you by electronic mail that a job is ready. Word processing then reviews and rearranges the document on the screen and sends back a finished product.

The decision has been made; you do not need approval to implement it. Draft a memo for Lotta Pages to sign.

6. PERCEPTION

The difference between effective and ineffective writing is usually found in the use of specifics. Too many people write about their vaguely formed opinions. Sharp writers go quickly to the point with clear descriptions of specific incidents the reader can see.

Appealing to the senses—plainly and clearly—strengthens your writing. Try this exercise. For half an hour, stay in one place recording only what you perceive, not what you conclude. Write only what the five senses tell you: sight, sound, taste, touch, smell. Do not say, "The park is fun." Say, "The sound of children playing filled the park."

People who do this exercise usually concentrate on sight with some sound. They do it in a park, a work lunchroom, or the backyard. Many people have had fun doing this exercise at a meal, although it is difficult to work both pencil and fork.

5.
Learn Less About Writing

Focused Freewriting

Remember freewriting. Now let's do something the same but different. It's "focused freewriting." Like freewriting, the idea of focused freewriting is to keep moving forward. Only this time, I will give a topic to write about (or "focus" on). It's takes about the same amount of time. Another aspect of focused freewriting is "loops." These are different ways of writing about the main topic of focused freewriting. Don't worry if it's not perfectly clear now. It's easy enough to master by following step by step. Let's do it now.

Step one: the topic
"Work." Write about work. Any thing about work. Any definition of work that matters to you. Inside the subject matter of work, all is open to you. Take about five minutes.

Step two: the first loop
Still within the topic of work, write about: "work at another time." Anything but now will do. Work in the 25th century. Work 500 years ago. Work at your first job. Any work except work now. Use your imagination. Take about five minutes.

Step three: the second loop

Write about work "to a child." Pick a specific child or children. Talk about work so the reader will understand. Take about five minutes

Step four: the third loop

Write about "a moment of work." Be specific. Select a particular incident or a certain day. Write about a real moment, something that happened. Write to the five senses: sight, touch, taste, hearing and smell. Sight is the most popular. Give me facts and details.

Step five: capture your experience

Think about what you have done and how you felt about it. Identify the problems you encountered. Then, more importantly, remember how you solved them to keep your writing moving forward.

By doing focused freewriting, you master the important skill of collecting initial ideas as they randomly enter your mind and stating them in a coherent fashion so the reader can see what you want to say. Note how each loop of focused freewriting is about the length of a typical memo. So how long does it take you to write a memo? About five minutes. You just did it. You also accomplished something important in each of the three loops.

First, you showed the ability to move out of the rut of everyday thinking. You brought a fresh perspective to the topic by writing about another time, something that most people do not do.

Second, you adjusted for a particular reader. Look at the language you used in writing to a child and compare it to the first focused freewriting on work. Note how it is different. But go beyond language. Didn't you take a whole new perspective in writing to a child about work? Perhaps you introduced the concept of going to a job. Maybe you compared work to school. Somehow you respected your reader enough to make the subject work for him or her.

Finally, you captured a specific incident. By focusing on a moment, you achieved a rare level of writing skill. Look at most of the writing where you work. What is it about? Vague concepts. The new sales theme. A particular management method. Rarely do people write about specific incidents capable of conjuring up a clear (and therefore memorable) picture in the reader's mind. You did.

Fast Tips composing
1. Using a word or phrase you hear only at work? Explain it immediately.
2. Write a first sentence less than two lines long.
3. Keep paragraphs to seven lines or fewer.

Each of the skills that you have demonstrated in this exercise is an important element of readable, productive writing at work. They will elevate your work above the mundane and make it stand out on a desk full of average writing, vague and disorganized.

Focused freewriting is the third of what I call the five fundamental writing experiences in this book. First you did freewriting and the unlocked door memo. Now focused freewriting. Each is a little different, varying in degrees of structure. Remember your experiences of each. Think about which type of writing experience suits you best.

Having tried out focused freewriting, you now can do it in many different ways. You can select all kinds of general topics and specific loops. General topics need to be broad enough to spark ideas. Some of the topics I have used in workshops include play, travel, vacation, rain, and any of the four seasons. The loops we used in this first exercise were carefully chosen, but there are many more. Vary the writer and the reader. Write about lies or first experiences. Again, a good coverage of focused freewriting is in the book *Writing with Power*.

Building on Fundamentals

Now that you have learned the fundamentals of process and know how you like to write, it is time to refine some skills. This next section highlights important ways to sharpen your writing.

You have no doubt already noticed my dislike of writing rules. However, one set of suggestions produced by one of this century's most powerful novelists can be useful. It is simple and comprehensive. After listing George Orwell's rules for better writing, the section quickly moves through other ideas for identifying specific writing problems and solving them.

George Orwell's Simple Rules for Writing

One of the problems I've always had with writing rules is trying to figure out how you use them. Do you write something down and then check it against the rules? Or do you read the rules before committing your ideas to paper (or screen)? Thinking about rules generally doesn't help people write.

That said, let me share with you four rules I like. They come to us from George Orwell. You remember him as the author of the novels *1984* and *Animal Farm*. If you think about those books, you will see both of them address the use of language. Orwell covered much ground in his writing (I recommend the story "On Shooting an Elephant."). A consistent theme throughout his work is how people use language. He found it powerful, able to manipulate large numbers of people.

To help move away from clumsy, insincere writing, in one essay, "Politics and the English Language," Orwell listed his six rules for writing. Each rule makes sense on its own. And as a group they give us a complete and comprehensive view of writing. Here are the rules.

1. Never use a metaphor, simile or other combination of words that you are used to seeing in print.
   [Never write, "It has been brought to my attention" or "thanking you in advance."]

2. Never use a long word when a short one will do.

3. If you can cut a word, cut it.
   [Or: When in doubt, leave it out.]

4. Prefer verbs in the active voice to verbs in the passive voice.

5. Never use a foreign phrase, a scientific word or a jargon word if you can think of an everyday English equivalent.

6. Break any of these rules sooner than say anything outright barbarous.

Aren't they simple? Once again the thrust of the message in these rules is to rely on yourself. Don't copy other phrases just because you have seen them often in memos; create your own sentences unique to your situation. Instead of using long words or complicated sentences in order to impress, write simply in plain language. Finally, be active.

That's it. The key to effective writing at work—as elsewhere—is sincere expression of what's in your heart. Most writers need to remove the clutter of bad habits rather than add any skill they currently lack.

The first three rules are easy enough to understand. The fourth takes a little work. Let's do that work now.

Using Active Voice

To liven up language, rely on what the grammarians call "active verbs." It is easy to tell the difference between active verbs and passive verbs once you look. Too often people slip into the habit of being passive with their verbs without thinking about it. Some examples illustrate.

Passive: The department <u>is supervised</u> by Jack.
Active: Jack <u>supervises</u> the department.

The verb—or action word—in each sample sentence is underlined. In the active sentence, a person is doing an action, supervising. The reader can see the action. In the passive sentence, the reader has more difficulty visualizing the action.

This example shows a typical solution to the passive problem. The sentence is switched around, with "Jack" moving from back to front. The next example is more involved.

Passive: Dead leaves <u>were scattered</u> on the ground.
Active: Dead leaves <u>covered</u> the ground.

Here, the writer has spotted a passive sentence and rewritten it completely. The active version is shorter and again more vivid. Notice also that the distinction between "active" and "passive" is not the same as action and no action. In the active version, the leaves are just as dead. Yet the construction of the sentence makes the meaning livelier for the reader.

Sentences beginning with "it" (or "there") often fall into the passive pattern.

    Passive: **It <u>was</u> not <u>anticipated</u> that interest rates would rise.**

    Active: **I did not <u>anticipate</u> interest rates would rise.**

More on active and passive

People often use the passive construction in writing at work on purpose to obscure who is doing the action. Look again at the example about anticipating interest rates. By using passive voice, the writer covers up the fact that he or she did not anticipate the rise in interest rates. A grammarian would recommend that the sentence be recast in active voice. Sometimes at work, however, writers do not want to commit to paper the details of a mistake. It is a trick you may want to use sometime. It is also a trick someone may want to use on you.

Passive verbs are not bad; they are just weaker than active verbs. They have uses. In the first example under the **Using Active Voice** segment, about Jack's department, for instance, if the passage were all about the department, the passive construction might fit in easily. You can also use passive when a subject is unknown.

The bill was corrected.

Perhaps the writer does not know the person who corrected the bill. The identity is not important. What is important is the disposition of the bill. Passive is often used when the writer wants to emphasize end results over human causes.

Profits are achieved by hard work.

The problem with passive comes when a writer uses it too much. It lulls readers to sleep. Generally, in a one-page memo, no more than two sentences should be passive. Those sentences should not be consecutive.

In a typical memo you write, how many sentences are active or passive? Do you have a memo you can evaluate sentence by sentence? If you have more than two passive sentences per page, can you justify them on the basis of the above examples, or do you want to recast them as active?

Stages in Writing, or the Only Work People do at the Keyboard Is Type

The typical image of a *writer* or of *writing* is someone sitting down at the keyboard (typewriter or word processor). But writing—especially at work—means much more than putting words down on paper. In fact, one of the most common problems people face is sitting down at the typewriter and waiting for *inspiration*. Unfortunately, many memo writers find out too late that the muses are so busy inspiring poets and novelists they never find time to visit memo writers. Writing means work. At work, when we say "writing" we usually mean an activity encompassing several people. They work together through these steps:

1. Researching and fact finding
2. Discussing the situation
3. Composing
4. Typing (by the writer or another)
5. Revising
6. Editing (optional)
7. Gaining approval or review
8. Sending it out.

Determine up front—in a way that is clear to everyone—who the "writer" is, the one who does the composing, the boss who approves it or the person who suggested the idea in the first discussion.

Revision

After you have written your memo, letter or report, you should go over it closely to make sure it does what you want. Revision divides into three distinct parts.

1. Revise for Content

Does it include an action statement or other summary? Does it include the facts that prove your main point? Are these facts accurate, especially the numbers? Is there a passage that clearly explains what it all means to your reader now?

2. Revise for Order

Do you state your point at the beginning? Is background placed where it makes sense to describe today's situation? Is the action statement at the end? (Sometimes, when you find an action statement buried in the middle, you can leave the statement there and then repeat it again at the end.)

3. Revise for Language

Are the commas placed correctly? Do any of the passages sound awkward? Is my spelling correct beyond a shadow of a doubt? Double check any unfamiliar names. Do all the pronouns clearly refer to nouns?

The key to successful revision is knowing when to do it. Many people suffer from the problem of revising themselves out of existence: as they think of something to say, they immediately decide it is not good enough so they write nothing. Separate revision from writing. Write it down first. You can change it later.

Exercise

Change the following seven sentences to active voice. For a look at possible responses, see Appendix I.

1. The copier is being used by too many people.

2. Several issues concerning the proposed development were raised by neighbors and representatives of the water district at the hearing held in September.

3. Completion of the program is projected to take place in 2002.

4. The department's productivity and its characteristics are presented in Figure 2.

5. The lake is recharged by ground water as well as by the creeks in the area.

6. For people preparing for a managerial career, promotions are being made faster when they include an educational component to their resume.

7. Commitment to excellence is shown by hard work and diligence.

6.
Better Letters

A Look at Your Letters

Let's take a look at your letters to see what is happening. Here's a handy checklist:

1. Are most of your letters less than one page long?

2. Do you keep paragraphs short (less than 10 lines)?

3. Do you rely on such phrases as "We are in receipt of…" or "This letter is in reference to your letter of…"?

4. Do you paraphrase laws and procedures, or do you play it safe by citing them word for word?

5. Do you use personal pronouns freely, especially "you" and "your"?

6. Do you address people by name ("Mr. Jones," "Joan Smith") rather than refer to them by their role in a procedure ("claimant," "credit applicant")?

7. Do your letters sound like the way you talk?

8. Do you answer a question before explaining the reasons or giving the background?

9. Do you automatically cut such phrases as "attention is called to the fact that," "it is noted," or "please be advised"?

10. Do you write the words most people use rather than the official terms such as "pay" instead of "disbursement"; "help" instead of "assistance"; and "new part" instead of "technology enhancement"? Everybody's answers to these questions are different. The important thing about answering these questions is learning more about how you write letters. As you work down the list you will be able to spot aspects of your letter writing that you will want to improve. It's up to you.

Letters are More Personal than Memos

A memo, of course, goes to people who work for the same organization as the writer. A letter does not. Since you send a letter to someone outside your organization who does not necessarily share your goals, the first job is to form a bond. If the letter concerns a previous sale, then the transaction can serve as this bond. Otherwise, the letter writer must create a personal bond with the reader before effective communication can take place.

Beginning a letter is one of the most difficult writing problems at work. Referring to an earlier meeting or an accomplishment of the reader can create the personal bond. Sometimes the writer has to acknowledge that the writer and reader have not yet met but may some time. (Answer the question, "What other communication is involved?")

Because of this need for a personal bond, letters are a more natural opportunity than memos to express the writer's personality. Feelings, beliefs and outlooks are more likely to affect letters than memos—both those of the writer and the reader.

While LEB123S serves as an effective format for many letters, it relies more on facts than is called for in many letter writing situations. A more common format, *AIDA*, often gets the letter message across better. AIDA stands for "attention, interest, desire, action." AIDA is a valuable format for sales letters.

Heavy on feelings and light on facts, letters following the AIDA format set up further communication so you can flesh out the details later. Sales letters are often the first step toward a phone call or sales presentation.

The following pages, a handy reference tool for the future, outline how to use the AIDA format in your letters. Then information on collection letters will help people who face this unfortunate writing task. Finally, exercises allow you to practice your new letter writing skills.

"To Randall Piersault, vice-president for Mergers and Acquisitions. Dear Randy: Shall we dance?"

Persuasive Letters

The following check list is not about your letter. It is about you. You don't have to include all the points mentioned. The list stimulates your thinking and reassures you that you have covered the necessary points. So here are some ideas for putting together a persuasive letter in any situation.

Attract the reader's *attention*

- Warm personal statement
- Comment on his or her situation
- Something the reader agrees with
- News relevant to the reader
- In response to a complaint:
    acknowledge a legitimate reader need;
    thank the reader for his or her suggestion
    thank the reader for getting involved
- A benefit to the reader
- Show concern for the reader's situation
- Refer to past action.
    RESULT: Reader decides to continue reading now.

Show why the reader has an *interest*

- Identify a particular problem or common concern
- Say why you are writing now
- Present the facts of the matter
    how your product or service works
    what your problem is
    mention possible benefits

- Prove statements made in the first section.

  Includes facts and figures

  RESULT: Reader decides you have credibility so he or she considers the message.

Appeal to your reader's *desire* to reach a goal

- Tell the end result of product or service—the ultimate benefit
- Include outside endorsements
- Ignore small objections; show why large objections do not apply in this case; acknowledge other objections
- Mention secondary benefits or future benefits
- Identify any enclosed materials or explain how to find additional information

  RESULT: Reader feels comfortable with you and wants to cooperate.

Describe exact *action*

- Show confidence but avoid hucksterism
- State clearly how your product or service will help the reader achieve his or her goal
- Even in a difficult situation always leave the reader with some recourse, never "take it or leave it"
- Match action statement with opening statement.

  RESULT: Reader takes the action you want.

Letters, more than any other aspect of writing, demonstrate the need to understand your writer. When writing a letter, you should have a clear idea of how he or she *responds* to each of your points. See how the results of each point are not about the letter but about your reader.

You may feel tempted to begin a letter with a question. That's okay. But I never do it. Questions are too dangerous because you do not know the reader's response. If I have trouble beginning a letter, I study the list under point one. If all else fails, especially if I am writing to someone I do not know, I have begun letters with this statement:

> "We have not had the opportunity to meet, but I look forward to...."

This opening is true and sincere.

Sometimes people want to begin with a question. There probably is no rule against it. But you have to do it carefully. Everybody knows you do not begin with a letter with a question that stimulates a "no" response. Not: "Do you want to be sad and lonely?" Yes: "Do you want to be happy and popular?"

One of the problems people create by trying to make sure the answer is "yes" is writing something phony that turns the reader off. I have seen too many variations of this kind of opening question: "Do you want to make money?" Of course, the answer will be yes. But people are not stupid. The excessively broad nature of the question invites reader skepticism. The best opening question matches exactly the needs of the individual reading the letter (not the needs of the writer). An effective opening question is usually unique to that reader and that situation. Again, imagination (with hard work) overcomes obstacles. With questions, be careful.

In the third section, you appeal to the reader's emotions. That scares some people who want to be business like and objective. Being too mushy or overly personal can be a problem at work. But in today's workplace, people emphasize interpersonal relations and the well being of others. That means acknowledging their emotional needs. So much for their point of view. From your point of view, you will only succeed in getting them to take the action in point four if you recognize both the thinking side of their personalities and the feeling side. When readers act, they do so as full persons, indivisibly intellectual and emotional at the same time.

The most effective way to think about the "emotional appeal" is to answer this question: "Why does taking the proposed action make the reader happy?" Typical appeals are to career advancement, ease of work or admiration from others. No need to go overboard.

Sometimes, however, the emotional appeal is negative. Often that is the case with a public agency. The government official writes to say that if you do not move your junky car from the street, the city will tow it away. The emotion the writer appeals to is fear. That's okay, but it is all the more important that the reader *immediately* learn exactly how to avoid the negative. Too often a letter begins with a description of the bad thing and withholds the action statement to the end.

On occasion, you have bad news. People don't like to say bad news but they really, really, really hate to write bad news. So what they do is torture the reader. The letter begins with compliments, tells the reader wonderful things throughout and almost as an afterthought delivers bad news bluntly at the end. This approach spares the writer's feelings, not the reader's.

Yes, it's probably not a good idea to baldly state bad news in the first sentence. But it's best to make the point quickly. As the AIDA format suggests, begin with a warm personal statement, then state the facts. Here's an example:

> Thank you for the clear, professional proposal you sent us regarding your services. However, we have decided to take the approach offered by ABC Associates.

Note also how this message is positive. The writer does not reject the reader but states the matter in terms of positively accepting another proposal.

Successful Sample Letter

The letter in the following section illustrates the AIDA format (Page 65). Within the first three words, the letter writer is discussing a subject of interest to the reader. This correspondence is a "blind contact," where there has been no previous contact between the writer and the reader. Since the writer could not refer to a previous meeting, he decides instead to begin with a benefit to the reader, a product that "practically sells itself."

Only after capturing the reader's attention does the writer describe the product he hopes eventually to sell. Notice how the writer expresses his subject from the reader's viewpoint ("clutter on your sales floor").

By the beginning of the fifth paragraph, the writer knows he has provided enough information for the reader to understand the facts of the product (a brochure, which responds to both question five and question six from the eight basic questions, accompanies the sales letter). Now he must address the reader's emotional reluctance. From experience, the writer knows retailers don't like old-fashioned wire racks. After bringing the subject to the surface, he connects his product with "beauty and charm." The money back guarantee, an emotional appeal to overcome fear, completes the segment.

The final paragraph states the exact action the writer wants the reader to take: "send for free information." The writer does not plan to make a sale on the basis of one letter alone. Although it is not stated in the letter, part of the writer's plan is to call later, knowing the letter has prepared the reader for the sale. The writer also adds a personal touch by once again mentioning to the reader the most beautiful word in the English language, her name.

Natural Manufacturing Company
1 Assembly Lane
City, State 10101   **(111) 555-1234; fax 555-4321**

Month, Day, Year

Louise Wong
The Retail Outlet
1776 American Way
City, State Zip

Louise,

    You have one of the busiest and most successful shops in your mall. You didn't get where you are by letting your stock sell itself. You understand the value of attractive presentation.

    The Selz-it display rack from Natural Manufacturing picks your products off the shelf and puts them eye at level for your customers. They see your full selection of products as soon as they walk in. The rack also helps you keep track of inventory. At a glance you see which items are running low and which ones are running slow.

    More clutter on your sales floor, you say? Not with Selz-it. At no additional cost to you, one of our representatives will show you how and where to install the right model to achieve the best sales results.

    Unlike the cheap wire rack found in many stores, Selz-it adds beauty and charm to the Retail Outlet's show room with its original and elegant design. Best of all, if you are not completely satisfied after using Selz-it for six months, you can return it at no cost.

    So if you want to boost sales and improve the appearance of your shop, Louise, send for free information about Selz-it. Or, you can call me directly to talk about how to display your products better.

Regards,

Glen Haven
Glen Haven

"Ms" taken Identity

Careful writers address each letter accurately. By spelling the reader's name correctly, including the exact job title and stating the full and correct company name, the writer immediately shows diligence and respect.

Part of accurate address is the proper use of a courtesy title. Men have only one such title, "Mr." Doctors, of course, prefer "Dr." You can find other formal titles in common reference books. Women use several courtesy titles, "Mrs.," "Miss," or "Ms."

Know Your Reader

Selecting the correct courtesy title is no different from other parts of writing. Reader point of view is the determining factor. Use only the courtesy title the reader prefers. It is not safe to refer to every woman as "Ms." Individuals have preferences. Some women strongly object to "Ms.," a term with political connotations they may not share. To communicate effectively with people, it is important to recognize their preferences in all matters, but especially when it comes to their names.

A surprising number of first names commonly associated with men now belong to women. Many people are already careful about Kelly, Robin, Jan, Pat, Leslie or Kim. But what about other names crossing the sex barrier such as Michael, Larry and Neville? These considerations point once again to the importance of knowing the answers to the *Eight Questions* before writing anything. Number two is, "Who is reading this?" It is usually worth the time and effort to call someone's workplace to double check spellings and job title before writing a letter. You can ask for the personnel department (human resources) in large organizations. When you state your purpose, people are usually happy to give you the information you need. This extra work is worth the effort if it helps you avoid one incorrect word in the address block of your letter.

Options for the Opening Salutation

While this guidebook does not address the wider topic of workplace etiquette, it is worthwhile to take a moment to discuss some common concerns over the opening salutation, the "Dear" part.

"Dear" is a throwaway line with no meaning. Its place in working letters continues as a convention. You can safely use it all the time. Some writers, however, drop it altogether. Omitting "Dear" is more frequent on the less formal West Coast. In the East, writers use "Dear" regularly. Up-to-date style manuals include the latest practices on workplace etiquette.

One way to avoid both the "Dear" problem and the courtesy title problem is to drop the opening salutation entirely. Instead, some letter writers use a "subject" line similar to the standard memo format. The subject line follows a thorough and complete address block in the upper left hand corner of the page. The subject line fits where the "Dear" salutation usually is.

He or She or What?

A related concern for people is the use of male gender pronouns to refer to both men and women. Nearly everyone today recognizes the inaccuracy and disrespect of referring to all readers as "he." The problem comes in finding a suitable alternative. I recommend the simple "he or she." It is not as cumbersome as some claim; it is accurate, and everyone recognizes it. It is best not to use this phrase in several successive sentences because such repetition is confusing. The phrase does become cumbersome when one sentence includes both "he or she" and "his or her."

Other alternatives, all less satisfactory, include using the plural, "they" and "their"; writing to avoid pronouns altogether; or alternating "he" and "she." The practice of alternating the two pronouns, although evenhanded, can be confusing. Now completely out of favor is the hybrid "s/he."

Know Yourself

Like so many writing problems, the solution to identity problems does not lie in the words. To be effective communicators, we must delve into the real meaning. Deciding whether to use "Ms" or to say "he or she" is a small part of a writer's overall approach to others. If you are genuinely even handed and respectful of others, your feelings come through on the page naturally and easily.

Collection Letters

One of the trickiest messages to write is the collection letter. The writer does not get involved until there is already a problem. Organizations follow a wide variety of tactics to collect overdue payments. Tactics depend on amount owed, importance of the customer and the nature of the organization.

Fast Tips for composing

4. Include sentences beginning, "You will be interested because..." and "What this means to you is...."

5. Put people action in each paragraph.

6. Make a negative sentence positive.

7. Use no more than two commas in one sentence.

Plan collection letters thoroughly and connect them with the rest of the company, particularly the legal department, the finance department and any part of the operation that handles repossessions. The federal Fair Debt Collection Practices Act and several state laws prohibit harassment and other heavy-handed tactics to collect debt. Such laws only emphasize the need for careful writing. Your organization, depending on its needs and methods of operation, must define precisely what is an overdue account and what is an account requiring action as serious as a legal suit.

The most effective and common method is the collection series. The letters of a collection series are usually form letters, individualized to each account by inserting the customer's name. Here is how the series can work.

1. First Reminder

At a certain point an unpaid bill becomes "past due." Typically, the bill becomes past due once a standard pre-determined deadline has passed with no response. The deadline might be 10 days or 30 days after a regular monthly notice goes into the mail. Such a deadline may seem short. But in a well-designed collection series, quick action prevents further problems with many customers.

Friendly in tone, the first reminder letter assumes the customer is not aware of the bill and wants to pay. As with all collection letters, clearly state the amount owed and describe the action necessary to pay the bill so that your customer knows exactly what do. A first reminder letter may open with a statement like this:

"We have not received your June payment of $101. Has payment been overlooked?"

The reminder letter provides enough information to the customer sufficient to identify the debt owed. Supply such information in a helpful tone so that your customer can find the matching information in his or her file. It is appropriate to thank customers for their business because the purpose is to maintain goodwill. Most customers will pay. Some require a second letter.

2. Inquiry

Again after a pre-determined deadline has passed with no response to the first letter, a second letter goes out automatically. While not criticizing the customer or laying blame, the second letter assumes there is a problem in making a payment. If there is a policy on interest and penalties, explain it clearly.

After explaining exactly how much must be paid and telling exactly how to make payment, the inquiry letter asks if there is a problem. Do not suggest the customer feels dissatisfied with the product or service. The letter supplies a way to answer any questions, perhaps by giving the name and phone number of a service representative. At this point, you may find that you have made some mistake, either in billing amount or in not being aware of a complaint however valid. By offering the invitation to resolve problems, the second letter ensures that further inaction is not the fault of your organization or the result of honest misunderstanding. If you receive no response from a properly done inquiry letter, you know the customer is purposefully and knowingly refusing to pay. Such a stance then requires—and justifies—the next, more forceful, step.

3. Ultimatum Letter

The final letter in the collection series describes the action that must happen as a result of non-payment. While the tone is clear to the point of sternness it is not threatening. It again supplies information about the original bill such as date and invoice number. The letter states once again exactly how much the customer owes, including interest and penalties, and exactly how to pay the bill.

The letter reminds the customer of the writer's efforts to collect the bill and answer questions in two earlier letters.

Then the ultimatum says what will happen if the customer does not make payment. Usually a deadline is not stated; instead, the writer asks for payment "today" or "immediately." Then it states what the action is: referral to the legal department or a collection agency; report to credit authority; legal action; repossession or loss of collateral.

Then take action. To avoid action is to invite both non-payment and further time loss on past-due accounts. By having a collection series worked out in advance and stored in word processing as form letters, you save much time. In addition, all customers receive the same treatment.

The "No" Letter

Often the goal of a letter is to say "no." This situation offers perhaps one of the few times when stating the main point immediately is not effective. Nonetheless, delaying the answer only builds false hope making the inevitable only that much worse. First be nice (yet truthful). Then say no.

Yours was one of the best proposals submitted for the project. We appreciate the time and effort you put into it, especially the color-coded sections. However, we have selected Ring, Dang, Do and Associates to complete the project.

Practice Letters for You to Write

1. TYPICAL LETTER

Identify a possible new customer or client. Write a one-page letter to that person. Decide what you want to do: get an order, inform, prepare the way for a phone call or something else.

2. REINFORCEMENT

Write a thank you letter to a current customer or client. (For social service agencies, write a positive re-enforcement letter.)

3. FORM LETTER

Write a form letter that you can send to any client or customer who has used your service or product for the first time. Assume you have word processing and can make variations for various products and services.

4. DON'T ASK WHAT'S UP

All the customers have to find out at the same time, says the boss, but each sales representative must notify his or her customers individually. You are a sales representative. Next week, your company is increasing prices. Your low end product, the flotsam, is going up 15 percent. The middle end product, the jetsam, is going up 7 percent. And the high end product, the lagan, is going up 5 percent.

Prices for the jetsam and lagan have not gone up for two years. The price of flotsam has not changed in five years.

Price increases have been caused by increased costs. Your customers are not expected to be familiar with the specific causes of cost increases. You have 47 accounts.

Write a form letter to customers telling them about the price increases. You have access to word processing. Mention the value of your product and reinforce your customers' desire to buy from you. Remind them of your attitude toward service.

5. NO

You work at the best public relations firm in your city. Many people want to work there with you. So many applications come in each day that no one can possibly read them all. However, your agency responds to each one. Write a form letter for unsuccessful job applicants where you work.

6. POOR PLANNING

You work for the land-use planning office at city hall. You just received a letter from Eliza Doolittle, who is mad at city officials. An insurance company has announced it is going to tear down an ugly, sterile office building and replace it with a pleasant looking apartment building that matches the character of the rest of the neighborhood.

Eliza knew nothing of this until she read it in this morning's newspaper. She sells flowers in front of the office building to business people. Apartment owners, she writes, won't buy her flowers. She wants to know why the city didn't tell her about the change.

In fact, your planning office bought a public notice in the daily paper six months ago when the insurance company applied to change the zoning to allow the apartment building. At one 7:30 p.m. public hearing, only two persons showed up besides the insurance company. At this time, it is perfectly legal for the insurance company to tear down the building and build an apartment complex.

Final design for the new building, however, must be approved by your office and then by the city council. The insurance company has not submitted plans yet so no official application process has begun. The city council meets every Monday at 7:30 p.m. It will hold a public hearing to take testimony on the building's design after councilors hear the recommendation from your office. Anyone can testify at that time.

Eliza did not include a request in her letter. Her final statement was, "This is the kind of no good junk I expect from you guys."

Write her a letter in response.

7.
Your Own Style

Develop Your Own Style

Writing has been called "the personality we create." By putting words down on paper, attaching our name and giving the final product to someone, we are saying, "This is who I am." This rarely acknowledged—but important—aspect of communication causes more worries about writing than vocabulary, grammar or punctuation. Use of language is the code we employ to express our anxiety over what people will think. These anxieties are often evident when more than one person works on a memo or report. ("This doesn't sound right," says the boss who reviews your work. "Check your grammar.") Worry is well founded. Whether we like it or not, people will judge us by how we write as much as what we write.

For many people, acknowledging that writing is creating a personality is a shocking prospect. That is because they do not know what to do about it. They are carpenters with plenty of lumber but no tools. But not you. You now command a format, you have already created a personal writing process and you know what works and what doesn't. So you are prepared to let your personality show through. Now is the time for style.

Often misunderstood because it applies to so many different aspects of writing, I use *style* here in the general sense. The word can apply to the small mechanics of writing; for instance, it is Associated Press style to lower case "a.m." and "p.m." Style can also refer to a consistent literary habit; Ernest Hemingway's style depends on short sentences. Do not confuse these uses of style, however, with another meaning of style.

This style is a sense of who you are. No effort will be made here to teach this type of style. Each person must determine that in his or her own way. Our purpose now is to recognize that such a thing as style exists for each person and to offer a way of selecting a personal style.

I like this word: *talkability*. It's not in your dictionary, but I bet you understand exactly what I mean. It's the quality of writing that makes it sound like talking. Writing that is easy to read aloud has talkability. It is simple, direct and natural, just the way you talk. In spoken conversation, you naturally say what is on your mind without feeling the need to outline, edit or revise. I like writing with that feel. Sometimes you have to work to make it feel that way. As any successful actor will tell you, you can't just be spontaneous; you have to practice it.

Talkability Exercise

Here are some typical phrases. Rewrite them to have talkability. Do that by making sure your final product has only one-and two-syllable words. Find possible responses (certainly not the only ones) in Appendix I.

1. Alternative approaches need your consideration. Past parameters do not match the requirements imposed by current conditions.

2. It is our expectation at this point in time that current company methodologies are sufficient for the near term. Accordingly, we envision no overriding need to prepare our staff for a transitional period as predicted in past outdated analyses.

3. For first-time travelers to the City of Nome, the most efficient business objective is the development of a set of characteristics based on the patterns of the indigenous personnel.

4. Production of graphics is a necessary stage for the successful presentation of work ideas in the large group or small group setting.

Fast Tips for composing
8. Write in present tense.
9. Appeal to one of the five senses directly at least once a page.
10. "Use a direct quote with quotation marks."

---

5. Specialization is no longer the most advantageous aspect of a management function. Rather, we should look for a broadly organized set of generalized skills as the designation of a good manager.

6. By interfacing the organizational development approach of my department with the technical expertise of your department, we can gain scheduling advantages.

7. The candidate for the position more than meets the functional requirements. Interaction with other staff, however, is a

consideration. In all likelihood, the candidate will overcome the obvious barriers to smooth interpersonal communications. This comment is designed to document possible problems so that they can be avoided and, if possible, eliminated altogether.

8. The office has maximized production, according to all of the usually recognized indicators. Consequently, if standardization were the ultimate goal, the situation would be normalized. Further inspection needs to be accomplished in order to be completely assured that actual capacity has been utilized in these unique circumstances.

Let's put it all together now. In the following exercise, write simply and naturally.

Return Letter to a Colleague
An Exercise

The following exercise presents several styles. Look them over to see which one applies to you. First comes a letter written to Lewis Cannon, vice president of Natural Manufacturing. Imagine you are in Cannon's place and have received this letter. However, you now must write a return letter turning down the offer.

You (as Cannon) have just joined the State Manufacturing Trade Council. Your membership in this small committee that oversees the activities of your trade association has not yet been announced publicly. The council will take all of your spare time. While you are attracted to the invitation from Melon, you know you will not have time to work on the commission, too. Yet Melon is a good customer of yours who has become a friend over the years. You do not want to risk alienating Melon.

Following the letter to Cannon are several possible return letters to Melon. Each has a distinct style. Is one style yours? How would you write such a letter?

Exercise steps

1. Read this page to learn the set up of the problem.
2. Read the letter on the next page. This letter is sent to you, Lewis Cannon, from your colleague Auguste Melon.
3. Write your response letter.
4. Study the three possible return letters on the following pages.
5. Determine what you like or dislike about each style. Apply the lessons we have discussed about adopting reader point of view and stating the main message clearly at the beginning. Do you see anything you want to adopt as part of your own style?
6. Read the comments on the next page.

A LETTER WRITTEN TO YOU

Lewis Cannon
Vice President
Natural Manufacturing
1 Assembly Lane
City, State 10101

Lew,
　　We need your brilliance once again. The state Economic Development Commission has a vacancy. In the time we've worked together, I have come to think you are the right person for this opening.

　　Sure it will look good on the resume. But we really need a person with hands-on manufacturing experience. We have some big ideas for turning things around. I know you will be more than a name on the letterhead if you join the commission.

Please let me know. I am counting on you.

Sincerely yours,

Auguste Melon

FIRST RETURN LETTER

Auguste Melon
Executive Director
Buyerton Industries
812 Hard Drive
City, State 10101

Mr. Melon,

Time pressures being as they are, we all have to parcel out schedule blocks on the basis of many priorities. With respect to economic development, nothing could be of higher interest. But interests cannot always be priorities.

Because of a previous commitment to the State Manufacturing Trade Council, it is not possible to attend both priorities. Regretfully, I cannot serve too many masters. It was nice to hear from you.

Regards,

Lewis Cannon

SECOND RETURN LETTER

Auguste Melon
Executive Director
Buyerton Industries
812 Hard Drive
City, State 10101

Auguste,

The state Economic Development Commission is an important agency with many responsibilities. Its members must devote time and attention to its many and varied duties.

Unfortunately, my present situation prevents me from dedicating the time necessary to complete those duties. As you may not know, I have accepted a membership on the State Manufacturing Trade Council.

My schedule does not allow me to carry out both responsibilities while still doing my job and addressing the needs of my beloved family.

But I am glad to see you are on the commission because I am sure you will serve ably.

Sincerely yours,

Lewis Cannon

THIRD RETURN LETTER

Auguste Melon
Executive Director
Buyerton Industries
812 Hard Drive
City, State 10101

Auggie,

Thank you for asking me to serve on the Economic Development Commission. I appreciate your kind words but I will not be able to serve with you because I have recently accepted membership in the State Manufacturing Trade Council. I just will not have time to work on both.

However, I am curious to hear some of your ideas for turning things around. The next time we get together, maybe we can discuss them.

Thanks again for thinking of me. Good luck.

Yours,

Lewis Cannon

Comment on Return Letters

First Letter

It begins with a statement so general it can apply to any situation, offering no usable information to the reader. Subject is about ideas, not people. Much passive voice. No personal words until the end. Response to the invitation, the information most important to the reader, is delayed. Sincere feeling of regret is obscured by use of cliché about "masters." Personal note at the end and warm close are semi-successful in belated attempt at a personal tone.

Second Letter

All facts. The opening subject of this letter is the commission itself, while the invitation letter was about Cannon's participation on the commission. No purpose is served by noting the fact that Melon is not aware of Cannon's new membership on the council. Sudden reference to family comes across as insincere. This insincerity then lessens the impact of the final sentence that would otherwise have been a friendly personable way to end.

Third Letter

Immediate answer to the invitation comes with a "you" word at the beginning. This letter acknowledges the "kind words" of the invitation instead of quietly accepting flattery. By picking up on the obvious excitement of Melon, letter writer keeps the relationship going with a comment on Melon's ideas for "turning things around." This letter recognizes that one of the topics of correspondence, besides participation on the commission, is the working relationship itself. Because the letter has been sincere throughout, it needs no additional personal comment at the end to reinforce the relationship, just a simple thank you and good luck.

Measuring Readability

One way to examine your writing microscopically is to apply one of the many reading ease measurements. These measurements count word length and sentence length. Then the two measurements combine to produce a final "reading ease" score.

These measurements are useful once in a while to get a thorough sense of your own writing. One reading ease measurement is relatively easy to use. It is the "Gunning-Mueller Fog Index" (a trademarked name).

Here is how to use it on a sample of your own writing at least 100 words long:

1. Figure the average number of words per sentence. Count the number of sentences in your sample. Count the number of words in those sentences. Divide the smaller number (sentences) into the larger one (words).

2. Compute the percentage of long words. Select the first 100 words of your sample. Of the words in this passage, count the number with three or more syllables. Don't count proper nouns such as names. Don't count words that have three syllables only because they end in "ed" or "es."

3. Combine the two values. Add the average number of words per sentence and the percentage of long words in the passage of 100 together. Multiply this sum by 0.4.

4. The result is your reading ease score. It is roughly equivalent to reading grade level. Remember, reading grade level does not

refer to the educational attainment of your readers or their intelligence. It refers only to how hard you make them work to get your message.

Most readers are comfortable reading at the seventh through ninth grade levels. Even people with college educations do not want to read memos written in a style that is as difficult as their college textbooks.

Don't put too much stock in reading ease scores. Use them to pinpoint specific problems. They might indicate your sentences are too long or your words are too long. To improve your reading ease level, shorten words or sentences.

8.
Resumes for Everyone

People write resumes for various reasons. Usually the reason is to find a job. A resume has a narrow, well-defined goal in the job search. It attracts attention for perhaps less than a minute for the purpose of stimulating the reader to call you to arrange an interview.

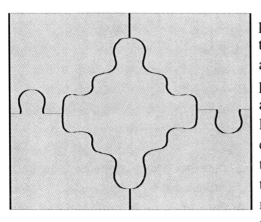

A resume, however, accomplishes other objectives outside the job search. The resume—and the thinking that goes into producing one—can be valuable for managing your career. Even if you are only vaguely considering a new job or a job transfer inside your organization, you can rely on the resume process to help you think through your plans. A resume is a valuable document for any person who takes his or her career seriously. It can serve as a reminder of what you have achieved as well as a guide to what you still want to accomplish.

Two reasons make writing a resume so difficult. First, you never know which parts of the resume will attract a particular reader so they all have to be outstanding, capable of promoting you quickly. Second, the subject of a resume is complicated and confusing: you. A resume purports to present an entire life in a page or two. That's why one page can take so long to produce. The life you are writing about is most likely one you are still trying to organize and understand yourself. That's why writing a resume produces so much anxiety.

Plan to spend some time writing yours. In a moment, you will see a process for identifying the information to include and for narrowing it down to its most important points. That process, by itself, should take two or three days of concentrated effort. If you are working and doing a resume in your spare time, the process should take at least a week of effort. Add in the time it takes to show somebody your resume to get a reader's response, and the whole process takes even longer.

The systematic approach I am about to outline is a basic one. You can use it today; you can use it five years from now. However, resume styles themselves change. One year a particular way of organizing information on a page is popular with human resources managers, and the next year it is no longer popular. Job hunting is competitive. When savvy competitors learn a particular way of doing a resume is successful, they adopt that method. Soon so many others are using the same method it becomes bland. Another way of doing a resume then becomes popular for a while.

After determining what you want to include in your resume and before you produce a finished product, you should learn what the current style is today in your field of interest. Many books on the subject are available. After checking with people who are in a position to know what is happening in human resources right now, read the currently successful books.

Regardless of how you choose to present yourself, certain points are necessary in a resume. Work history, education and job skills provide the foundation of any resume. In order to present this information and other supporting information in a way that is likely to achieve your purpose, you must know what you want to say. Instead of trying to write the ideal, perfectly polished one-line job history, take time to write more than what you will eventually include in a resume. Then focus on the best.

A Step-by-Step Way to Do It

1. Write down what you want to do in life.

By actually committing your life goals to paper, not only will you take an important step toward realizing them, but also you will have a chance to update them or change them to fit your current circumstances. Be expansive. Be unashamed. Write what you want in life—not merely the title of job, but a life. This step is fun.

2. List everything you are good at.

Start with job skills and qualifications but keep going. Do you have a winning smile? List it. How about a stylish tennis game? List it. Identify everything about you that you think is good and valuable regardless of what anyone else thinks. Even if you know you have potential in an area but have yet to show it, list it. Include hobbies. You will generate more ideas than you thought possible so take your time. Be thorough.

3. Prove you are good.

Now that you have listed what you believe you can achieve, show the outside world why it is true. Be specific. Write job achievements, contests won, compliments from others, successful job projects, published writing, classes, certificates, credentials, or particular achievements. This step is more difficult than the first two because it requires you to view yourself ruthlessly from an outside point of view. You had fun in steps one and two; now you sweat a bit.

4. Tie it together.

Looking over everything you have written, perhaps three to five pages, find the common strings. What themes show up in all three steps: you want to do it, you are good at it and you can prove it. If you are like most people, the common threads will follow a few areas. You may see achievements in step three that do not lead you to your life goals at all. Select as many "threads" as possible containing a goal in a field you are good at that you can prove with specific examples. You should see at least one, and maybe as many as five.

5. Describe work experiences.

Be concise but write enough to explain the job. Use the language of your chosen field or fields as much as possible. Include volunteer work. The most common organizational pattern is reverse chronology, latest job listed first. You do not have to follow that pattern. Now that you have identified some goals, you may want to list the most appropriate job first. It depends on your particular goals. Show time worked in terms of years only when possible. List months when necessary. Starting and ending days create confusing clutter.

6. Catalog education, formal and informal.

Describe precisely exactly what college degree you earned. Include miscellaneous classes along the way as well as non-credit classes from schools or other institutions.

7. Record military experience.

If you served only a couple of years, list dates and final rank. Write down promotions and achievements. If you have a military career, include this in your work description in step five.

8. List awards, community services and professional organizations.

This section is for meritorious distinction. If you have any acknowledgments, include them. Include services on a board of directors or neighborhood clean up projects. Repeat items that you may have recorded earlier. Include activities that you may have missed earlier. Be specific about times and locations.

Fast Tips for revising
1. Find all versions of the verb "to be."
Replace them with stronger verbs.
2. Rewrite all sentences beginning "It" or "There."
3. Change "could" to "can" and "would" to "will" or "want."
4. If you cannot explain the reason for using a comma, dump it.

When you have completed these eight basic steps, what you will have is a document five to ten pages long, depending on how you wrote it out. You will be surprised what you have learned about yourself. While working through this process, you may even change your mind about what you want to do. You may discover talents you never noticed. You may also find that you have a job objective in a field you do not much like. Hopefully, you will have reinforced and refined your original ideas.

This process tends to be very meaningful for people. It gets at the part of resume writing that so often produces anxiety. By mapping out a plan and organizing your positive experiences, however, you reduce the anxiety. Because this process is so meaningful, many people include their spouse or friends along the way for direction or just someone to talk to.

The written product at this stage is an important map of your life, outlining the paths already taken and connecting them to the road you have yet to travel. This document is valuable for future reference. Years from now, you may decide to engineer a career switch; the information you worked out in this process will help you decide. You may even look at the document and decide to drop out of the work world. Who knows?

Now you are ready to prepare the document usually called a resume—your career boiled down to one or possibly two pages. As discussed above, find out the current popular resume style. Are human resource managers looking for an "objective" on top this year or do they want to know your overall skills and experiences. Once you determine the most effective way to organize the information, you will easily be able to select the appropriate information to include. The information you write down in this resume process will be relevant no matter what fashions may currently be popular in the field of human resources.

Everything you have read earlier in this book about writing memos and letters applies to your resume: know your purpose, identify your audience, be specific, and the rest. Any expert in the field of human resources will suggest you show drafts of your resume to others for feedback. Do that and be prepared to make changes—even to your favorite parts. Remember the purpose of your resume. It is not to praise yourself but to stimulate someone else to want to know more about you.

Once you have come to grips with who you are and what you want to do, the polishing and honing of the resume will be simpler tasks. Finally, never expect to be done. People are rarely satisfied with how they present themselves on paper or otherwise. That's just life.

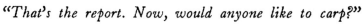

"That's the report. Now, would anyone like to carp?"

9.
Reports Without Boredom

A report is a management tool used to make decisions. When properly done, a report allows its reader to expand his or her scope of work. Reports can be internal—addressed to higher management—or they can be external such as proposals to clients. As mentioned earlier, for this book, the term "report" is any document longer than two pages. That is the length when most readers alter their reading approach. Instead of immediately plunging into the thing, as they would with a one-page memo or letter, they frequently devise a reading strategy. Maybe you recognize this common strategy: "I'll put this over here and read it tomorrow." A well-done report acknowledges reader strategies and puts them to work to make the document more useful. Where you work, you may use the term "report" differently. Perhaps people call a particular one-page memo the "monthly report." Fine. Just remember the point of this chapter is to improve your longer documents.

This chapter presents a solution so let's be clear on the problem. The problem is taking a long time and worrying a lot to produce a bunch of junk. Too often a writer defines a report only in terms of length and then goes out to compile as much information as possible to reach the desired length. The operating principle involved is, "If it's longer, it must be more important." The situation goes something like this: you have a month to produce a report so you immediately begin to collect information. Suddenly, much time passes (you had an unexpected interruption) and your report is due in two days. You haven't started writing it yet. Then you pack all the typing you can into two days, putting off other duties because the report is now an "emergency." After fooling with the printer to get your graphics right, you barely finish on time. You hand in a long document that reports everything yet says nothing.

Instead, from now on, let's master the report by breaking it down into stages. Here is the Six Stages of the Report:

Stage 1: What Am I Doing?

You complete a report successfully by dividing the work into stages. Naturally, as you well know by now, the most important factor is the reader. But to determine how best to serve the reader, you will need to determine a fundamental point in the first stage. The approach to researching, writing and presenting a report will depend on which one of these statements is true at the beginning:

1. I know my conclusion or
2. I do not know my conclusion.

Most of the time, especially for problem reports, the second statement presents the case. Often, a person writes a report because nobody knows answers to certain questions. It's all right not to know your conclusion at the beginning of the writing project. It's not all right at the end, however.

Stage 2: What Are They Doing?

In many ways, a report is like a memo—only more demanding. To begin a memo, you answer the *Eight Questions* of Chapter Four. Reports require answers to a similar list. More than memos or letters, a report meets particular specifications. Know them:

1. Who is reading this (by name and function)?

2. When do they want it?

3. How will it be used?

4. How long do they have to read it?

5. What are the rules and specifications—formal or informal?

6. Does this report convey information or recommend action?

7. If action is recommended, who is taking the action (reader, writer, third party)?

8. Who approves or reviews before the report is complete?

9. What other reports will the reader have (earlier versions on the same subject, reports from the writer's peers, past or future reports in a cycle, competitor reports)?

Stage 3: LEB123S Format Expands to Cover Reports

A long document requires an underlying structure to hold all those pages together and to present a coherent, memorable message to a reader. Otherwise, it's just a list—a long, boring list. The LEB123S format is even more important for a report than for a memo. Rarely would I deviate from this format in a long report. (I have broken the format before for certain reports but, as always, I broke the rules with full knowledge of what I was doing and why.)

Typically, a report begins with an introduction stating the main point and explaining why the writer prepared the report. Sometimes, the explanation includes how the writer compiled the report. An appropriate explanation might describe the methodology used to gather the facts: when and how. Or an explanation might tell who wrote the report, especially if it is the project of a committee or group.

A background may describe the problem the report is designed to address.

Reports Must Build on Facts

Examples are the heart of an effective report. Usually they take the form of a case study. Each example supports a particular conclusion stated in the lead. Too many reports are nothing more than facts. All kinds of facts. In fact, they aren't really a report so much as a list of research tidbits. The examples or case studies expand and amplify the conclusions set out in the lead. Each needs a clear point. The reader needs to be immediately clear on why each example is included. You may find that within a long example–such as a case study–you once again follow the LEB123S format. Begin the case study by stating the point, explain that point, give background on why you included this case study, offer the facts of the case study and summarize the specific point.

Sum Up the Next Action

And, of course, the summary says where we go from here. In some cases the action may be about the report. You may write a report to submit it to a reviewing agency or to support a project that now goes to the board of directors for consideration. Make sure all the readers you identified in the beginning understand your report's role in the review or whatever the next step is. A common form of action in long reports is a list of options or recommendations.

Poor reports are usually a multi-page mishmash of history, ideas, case studies and recommendations.

Reach a Conclusion

Sometimes, after a writer has done plenty of research, he or she will know exactly what conclusion to state in the lead. In such a lucky case, writing out the introduction is usually the best place for a writer to start.

But when a writer has not yet reached a conclusion—perhaps because of an abundance of research—this is when knowing a format is most helpful. Because the writer knows what the final, overall structure will be, it is not necessary to write the lead first. So an effective way for a writer to reach a conclusion is to detail each case study first. By focusing on the examples segment of the report, a writer can often think through to the best conclusion to put into the lead.

During large writing projects such as an important report, the writer who knows his or her own process and begins with a final structure in mind has the advantage over the person who is less organized.

Stage 4: Types of Reports

At this point, you have an outline and a general idea of what your readers are looking for. Now you need to sharpen your conclusion, either make it more relevant or decide what it is. That depends on the type of report you are preparing. Here are the common types of reports produced today:

1. Affecting Management Decisions

Examples: proposing a new idea, responding to management request, troubleshooting, conducting pure research.

Usually done by middle management or supervisors, these reports trail "up" the organizational chart. (In more modern organizational models, such reports may be done by a member of a working group for the benefit of peers within the entire group.) They need to provide readers with a full understanding of the situation. The writer is probably in the best position to recommend the desired action but is not the one who has the authority to take the action. A common problem is presenting the entire situation well enough before petering out at the end, leaving the reader with no idea of what action to take. Some people are afraid to recommend a clear, decisive action to the boss. Don't be. Managers sometimes request reports precisely because they know they do not have the best view of a particular situation. A deadline is sometimes most relevant.

2. Reviewing or Changing Operations

Examples: monthly sales, personnel, performance of product or a service (usually recurring).

Sometimes we have to know what's going on around here. The idea with this type of report is to present a clear picture of the people, procedures, successes and failures of the regular work. Both the writer and the readers are similar to the ones mentioned for the first type of report. The action statement, however, is usually less decisive and original. For example, the reader may want to know if sales are up or down over the past quarter. If the review presents a picture of general success, the action may be to let things alone. In the case of a specially requested, one-time review, sometimes called an assessment, the report is usually the beginning of a change. The reader needs to understand why the writer did the review and what is supposed to happen because of it.

3. Proposing New Business or Support

Examples: response to bids, application for charitable grant, new project for existing client.

The first two reports are internal. Not this one. That means your message must be sharp. You probably should be able to sum up your point in one sentence, like this: "Flambo, Inc., is the only company with the people and equipment necessary to meet the fast-track deadline for your project." Your whole report will be about that statement. Presentation is important. A catchy title and consistent theme line will differentiate you from the competitors. Flattery helps. That action statement needs to be a clear description of exactly what you want: the call for a sale or a request for an interview.

4. Documenting Work

Examples: monthly report to client, progress report, end of project report.

Heavy on the facts of the matter, this report often omits background and may even handle explanation in a sentence or two. As the examples indicate, this report is usually cyclical until the last one. View the report as part of long string beginning with the proposal or mission statement and building to the final one. Readers are usually involved and already generally aware of the situation but they are relying on the report for important documentation. The action statement can foreshadow the work for the next month or whatever the report cycle is.

5. Showing Compliance with Requirements

Examples: Compliance with government programs, quarterly summary of operations, annual reports.

"We will follow all the rules" is usually the action statement for this report. If the examples show that your organization has been complying all along with the laws or the contract stipulations, that action is a continuation of past practices. If the report reveals problems, the action statement details the steps taken to correct the problems. Background can be important in such reports, because what the reader does is measure current practice against paper regulations enumerated in the past. These reports tend to be perfunctory, not leading to any changes in operation. An exception is the annual report, which can be a valuable document for many organizations, not just those required to issue one to stockholders. Annual reports can be the cause of news coverage. The document itself can accomplish year-long public relations goals by becoming the support document for many types of presentations. If you want to use the annual report in this way, you need to coordinate the message and presentation with the organization's entire communication plan. Professional help is usually worth the cost.

6. Establishing Policies or Procedures

Examples: Employee benefits program, company policy on quality assurance, major change in operations.

After a decision has been made, a report sometimes conveys it to a larger audience. This type of report usually comes after the managers and others have mulled over the first type of report. Action statements here are huge. The point of the report is to implement change such as a new health plan. Background must provide credibility for the changes. Americans won't take your word that they need to do something different now; you have to prove it to them.

By picking one type of report and sticking with it all the way, you greatly increase your reader's chances of understanding what you have to say.

Stage 5: Discovery

Confused about where to start with research? Most people are. Ignore that. You do not need to have a plan to begin research. Just start. After a while a pattern emerges. One or two areas stand out as important. Something that seemed important at first becomes too difficult to learn about. Drop it. Something that seemed minor blossoms into a major topic.

The idea is *not* to organize, then research. Instead, research, organize and research again. If you have determined a format, if you know what type of report you are writing and if you know what your reader needs, the report begins to write itself. The following lists stimulate ideas of where and how to find information for a report.

Here are types of information that contribute to a report:

- Overview of what has happened before
- Changes expected in the next year (or in the next budget cycle) that affect your organization
- Explanation of how information was gathered and selected
- Any scientific, professional or statistical methods used to analyze raw information or conclusions
- Social, political and economic trends foreseeable in the next five years, some happening in your local community and some happening in the larger society
- What your organization has tried before in this area
- What competitors are doing or may do
- Related successes
- Related failures (objections to overcome)
- What other departments have to say
- Obvious opponents and supporters of an idea
- Recommendations, conclusions, proposals, options.

Here are research methods to find information:
- • Personal contacts in the community, in the industry or in another part of the organization
- • Interviews with people in a different department familiar with the topic (such as customer service representatives)
- • Phone calls and letters (find or keep a log)
- • Field reports
- • News media reports
- • Annual budgets and budget requests
- • Previous reports
- • Internal computer data bases
- • Commercial computer data bases
- • Census
- • Surveys, opinion polls and questionnaires
- • Idea juries such as an organized discussion at lunch
- • The public library (books, magazines, research directories).

As you research this type of information from these sources, remember how you have organized your report process in stages one through four. Write as you go. For example, if you are suggesting an idea that has been tried before, you will have to describe the first try. That's probably background. Write it and plug it into your format knowing a lead and some case histories will soon surround it.

A common failing of reports is lack of a crisis point. This type f report is just a big list of stuff. The writer does not make clear the central point of the thing. Successful reports answer the question, "What do we do now?" Your reports need to make clear why now and what will happen if action is not taken (always a possibility). For a report to be worth reading, it must revolve around a central issue that affects people. That's the crisis point.

A crisis point frequently revolves around money. A decision that most managers make is whether to repair machinery or replace, a good topic to assign to a staff member for a report. In this circumstance for example, the writer builds to this crisis point: "It is more cost effective to repair the equipment for the next year, rather than to replace it." The crisis point makes the report worth reading.

It is not worth reading a report that simply suggests spending money to make improvements. It is always possible to find something to buy that will help do the job better. The question will always be, is the cost worth the improvement. Organizations operate in their own kind of balance. A good report identifies the point where the organization moves out of balance, either toward improvement or toward deterioration.

Stage 6: Present It

Successful reports match readers with entry points. You already know what readers are. Let's talk about entry points. Everybody knows one entry point, the beginning. Nearly all reports assume the reader starts at the beginning and proceeds forward. Yet they hardly ever do.

The nature of reports is that they have a variety of readers with a variety of needs and goals. Since most writers think about subject instead of reader (but not you), they fail to distinguish the various needs of readers.

Other entry points are section headings, the conclusions or recommendations section, the table of contents, a summary (forget the "executive" part) and beginning of the case studies, your examples.

Make sure you know all your readers and understand how they will read your report, especially where they will start. For example, the president of the company may not want to read the examples but will go immediately to the recommended actions. A department manager may want to know the whole picture and therefore begins with the executive summary. The subjects of the case studies will want to know the factual basis of the report so they will read the examples first.

Capture each reader's attention at the beginning of each of these general entry points. In addition, each report—especially a long one—needs its own particular entry points. Highlight the beginning of sections especially important to your organization or particularly relevant right now.

Let's Do It

From today's paper, select one article that you can condense into one example or case study of a larger report. Write no more than one typewritten page. Make sure to be clear on your general proposition.

Making Your Reader's Work Easier

Readers devise a strategy for reading anything longer than two pages. That's what makes these document reports. Help them with their strategy. Use what I call "road maps" to explain how they can use the material in the report. The explanation often serves as a road map to the whole report, explaining how the writer put information together and telling the reader precisely where to find specific information.

Sprinkle sentences throughout that keep the reader informed of the plot line. Recap the past: "Now that you have a firm grounding in how we got this far, let's take a look at some ways we can respond." Introduce long sections by warning what is coming: "On the following four pages you will see the results of the first experiment we conducted last year."

Recognize the varied experience of readers: "If you have been following this subject, you may want to skip the next section. If you want background, the section helps you understand the recommendations."

Always keep a dialogue going with your reader. Remember—this is especially important for long documents—the subject is never the technical information. It is always how the technical information affects the reader's life. Take a look once again at the three sentences in quotation marks ("Now that you…" "On the following four…" "If you have been…"). Note how they are not about the report. The road map sentences are about the reader reading the report.

Headings and Stuff That

The common tool for both entry points and road maps is section headings. The key here is consistency and simplicity. Since you already have your format, you are clear on the best place for headings. But don't make the mistake of simply saying "Background." Put the heading to work for you by adding information: "Background: A History of Incompetence, Stupidity and Lust."

An unfortunate byproduct of computer word processing is too many options. It is now possible to place a dozen different typefaces in a report. Variety does not show creativity. Have a reason for all typefaces. The most readable typefaces, good for body text, are in the Times Roman family. They have the little squiggles on the letters that draw the reader's eye forward. Big, bold headlines can be in the clean Helvetica type. Add bold, italic and underline (rarely) cautiously and consistently. Design enhances message; it cannot substitute for a message that is not there.

Heavy Lifting: Defining Terms, Attributions, Citations, Appendices

People often debate whether to use footnotes or endnotes. I don't have the answer. That depends on each individual situation. The answer will come from your readers. Rely on the format that makes their reading strategies easiest. Many style manuals are useful. I prefer the Gregg Reference Manual.

Visual Aids

Use charts and graphs as necessary, not for art. Each should be able to stand alone as complete thought. The use of graphics is rapidly changing because of new computer programs for word processing and for page layout. For that reason, I have decided to skip over how to actually present charts and graphs. You can find the most up-to-date 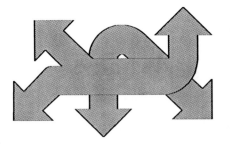 and valuable information for your needs in your word processing manuals. More than the rest of your information, visual aids are about the reader, not the material. The purpose of a visual aid is to interpret information into a language that the reader more easily understands. Some people like charts and some don't. Make sure you know your reader before including one. If you are having trouble typing out such information, it usually means the graphics are more bother than they are worth.

One type that remains valuable, however, is using white space. Do not assault the eye with large blocks of type. Long reports may require a whole page covered with body text. Most do not. Add white space at section headings. Use subheads when possible to relieve the eye.

Teamwork

Fast Tips for revising
5. Replace each word ending "ize" with a shorter one.
6. Cut "ly" words.
7. Make sure each page has at least two short sentences less than one typed line. If not, cut a long sentence in two.
8. Identify each paragraph as an element of LEB123S.

For many organizations, a team gathers to produce a report, especially a proposal. Too often I have seen most of the team's time wasted in getting organized and trying not to work at cross purposes. You can tell if you have an organized team working on a proposal by how you review the document before the final presentation. If the last stage is simple proofreading, you are putting together the type of boring list of words we discussed at the beginning of this section.

However, if your team conducts a focused review designed to make sure the final product matches the initial goals, you are putting together a project that meets the reader's needs. Do you review the decisions you made in stages one and two to make sure the report meets the initial goals. If the report precedes a presentation to the management or a client, design it with the presentation in mind, especially who will present what and in what order. Fit the report to the overall strategy of the project.

The way to make best use of the team is to understand the underlying structure. You do. Make sure each member recognizes the LEB123S format. Have all agree in the beginning on the answers to the questions you raised in stages one and two. Assign segments based on the format. One person collects background, for example, while another bangs out the case studies. The single greatest value of the universal format for many workplaces is that it gives people a language for communicating what they are trying to do. As a team, they move away from the goal of writing until it "feels right." And you move to the goal of hitting "defined standards."

Performance Review

Facts. A performance review functions at work like any other report. The distinguishing feature of a performance review, however, is fact. The standards for factual information in a performance review are higher than in most documents. For instance, a manager usually should not say, "The employee is late often." The manager should say, "The employee has been late six times in the past three months." Better yet, if possible, the manager should mention the dates when the employee was late.

Time To Be Precise

The obvious reason for such precision is that the exact information is stronger in case of a dispute of a review. However, precise facts are also useful with any employee to provide direction and guidance. Positive information should also be factual. Additionally, the formal performance review is supposed to provide a benefit that daily management does not. The formal written review communicates exactly what a manager expects without the clutter of other projects happening at the same time or the constraints caused by a lack of time.

For performance reviews, local rules apply. Make sure your performance reviews use the same language as the rest of the organization, especially previous managers in your position or managers in similar positions.

Use Format Variation to Organize

Because practices are different in various organizations, it is difficult to provide universal guidelines for performance reviews. Some reviews are given yearly and therefore are long and detailed, while others are given quarterly and contain a few brief comments. Yet what is usually required in a performance review is a lead with two or three specific examples. Background is rarely necessary if the individual review is part of a long-running personnel file. A general statement followed by specific incidents is most efficient.

The employee has a tardiness problem. She was late at least once a month this past year, including two times so far this month.

In this example, the first sentence is a lead. The second sentence is two examples. Depending on circumstances and the nature of the performance review, the manager may include an action summary:

She is expected to maintain at least 40-hours a week each week on her time card.

With this sentence, the employee knows precisely what you expect from now until the next performance review. Misunderstandings can be cleared up immediately.

This example focuses on a negative comment. The same standards and practices apply to positive comments. Note the following example using the same format—lead, two examples, action summary:

During the probationary period, the employee has consistently completed projects on time. The Johnson project was completed a week early. And although the Smith project was done a week after the initial deadline, the employee reported problems beforehand and met the revised deadline. Now that probation is complete, the employee is expected to assume the standard workload of the office, which is two completed projects a month.

Subjects to Cover

Many organizations have standard forms for presenting performance reviews. If your organization does not, here are standard subject areas for providing employee evaluations:

- amount of work
- quality of work
- ability to follow direction
- ability to direct the work of others
- initiative
- reliability
- relations with other workers
- relations with customers
- future role with the organization.

One way to do an effective employee evaluation is to list strengths and weaknesses under a variety of subject headings. Every subject does not have to have both strengths and weaknesses, but every applicable subject needs a comment. Some subjects may not apply, such as "ability to direct the work of others." List strengths first.

Content and tone of written performance reviews are important aspects of maintaining an effective, humanistic work environment. The rules of simple courtesy along with standard management principles and guidelines for interpersonal communications apply. These standards and guidelines are available from a number of sources. They include such points as criticize the behavior, not the person; know your facts; do not act in haste; do not ridicule; share responsibility; include both positive and negative comments; maintain a friendly tone, especially in the final comment.

Writing Sample Reports

1. QUALITY

Find one aspect of quality for your customers or clients. Define. Report on which departments affect it and how. Suggest improvements or further methods of discussion and examination.

2. NEWSPAPER SUMMARY

Read page one of today's newspaper. Report to the head of your organization what happened. Explain the news in terms of how it affects your organization or how your organization might affect something in the news report.

3. MEETING REPORT

Get the printed minutes of a meeting. Select a manager who has an interest in the meeting—perhaps the manager of the department where the meeting was held. Make a report to the manager. Determine which of the six types of reports you are writing.

4. WHAT IS A CUSTOMER?

Your boss wants to know the difference between the people who become customers and the people who hear a sales pitch and don't become customers. She needs a report to give to the board of directors at the next quarterly meeting two months from now. She drops the problem in your lap. How do you find out the information? How do you organize the report? What is the action statement for such a report? Don't write the report on the customers/not customers thing. Write a shorter report to your boss about how to construct the work project to produce the report the board of directors wants to see.

5. RESEARCH METHODS

What research methods would you use in each of the following situations?

a. Your company manufactures lawnmowers. You sell only to distributors who then wholesale to retail outlets. Your products retail under four brand names, including three house brands. The marketing manager wants to find out the single most important reason for buying the premium lawnmower.

b. Same company. The manager of manufacturing wants to know the most common reason for a breakdown.

c. You work in an office supply company in a medium sized city. You have three retail outlets. Historically, the big competition has come from your cross town rival. You maintain roughly equal market shares. Other competition includes grocery stores and a couple of smaller shops. A big national chain is thinking of opening a store in your area. Your boss says to you, "Find out what people think of us."

d. You repair buses for a transit line. You notice that over the past two months, more buses than ever before are having trouble with brakes. Nobody else has noticed this yet. You want to write a report to your supervisor explaining the problem.

e. Your company of 150 people in three locations has selected a new health care plan that is scheduled to begin in four months. What is the best way to let your employees know?

f. How well did your place of work perform compared to the same quarter last year?

g. What is the average length of employment where you work among senior managers, middle managers and line staff?

h. You work for your city's local planning bureau. Over the past five years, you notice an increase each year in lawsuits against your regulations. You usually win them. But you think a citizen review committee will prevent costly legal negotiations. You want to recommend the change to your boss, the planning manager.

i. Last year, your company, the third largest insurance carrier in the state, dropped its "total quality management" program after trying for two years. You think you know why the program didn't work and you want to try it again. You are the director of the Department of Human Resources, reporting directly to the CEO.

10.
Achieving the Next Level

Signs of Excellence

Now you understand how to organize any memo, letter or report. You command the basics that put you ahead of three-quarters of the people writing at work today. Two more techniques, once you master them, will further distinguish your writing as excellent. They are parallelism and sentence variety.

Parallelism applies to parts of sentences used in a series. Words, phrases and clauses must follow identical structure so the reader can follow the meaning without distraction. Let's go through several examples to illustrate how parallelism works. We begin with sentences that suffer from lack of parallelism.

Parallelism

Example #1
The majority of my work consists of memos, in-house and to distributors.

This sentence ends with a two-part series describing types of memos: "in-house" and "to distributors." These phrases are not parallel. The first is a hyphenated word and the second is a prepositional phrase with two words. To understand parallelism it is not necessary to know grammatical rules. I am sure you can see the sentence is not parallel without knowing what a prepositional phrase is. (More on grammar follows in the Usage section.)

Several changes can make this sentence parallel. One solution is to replace "in-house" with "to other employees." Now the two types of memos are each described by a phrase beginning with "to." The meaning of the sentence comes across more clearly to the reader because he or she naturally expects the structure of the second phrase to match the structure of the first. When the sentence follows the expected parallel structure, the reader understands the writer's meaning without the distraction of uneven structure.

Now we move to a longer series of phrases requiring parallelism.

Example #2

The most important parts of my job are to talk with people coming to the office, to keep track of sales orders and arranging sales meetings.

The second example illustrates of perhaps the most common error in lack of parallelism. The sentence ends with a series of three items listing the important parts of a job. They are "to talk," "to keep track," and "arranging." By the time the reader reaches the third item, he or she is expecting to hear another phrase parallel to the first two that began with "to."

The solution is simple. The word "arranging" substitutes for "to arrange." Parallel. Can you hear the difference this substitution makes? Cultivate that sense of sound in your writing. Another solution is equally successful. The first two items can change to match the third, substituting "talking" for "to talk" and "keeping track" for "to keep track." Also parallel.

Example #3

The customer for this product is the person who wants to start on the system for the first time or is already a user and wants more information.

The third example is more difficult. However complicated this sentence may seem on first reading, the basis of the problem is lack of parallelism. Notice how the sentence sounds better once you insert a second "who" in front of the word "is." Can you see other ways to improve this sentence by using parallelism?

Example #4

I am frequently on the phone with co-workers tracking orders, checking parts availability and progress on new equipment design.

Here is an example for you to practice on. By applying what we have discussed so far in parallelism, you should be able to spot the problem and improve this sentence by making it parallel.

Example #5

The most effective people in any organization are those who find out exactly what management expects in each aspect of the job, who set and stick to long-term goals and who learn what their co-workers expect of them.

The fifth sentence is an example of how parallelism works for you. Although the longest of these examples, this sentence is easy to understand because three long clauses each begin with "who." Parallel construction alerts the reader to what to expect.

Example #6

My job consists of taking orders, delivering equipment and making sure customers follow the proper maintenance plans.

This last sentence shows how to use parallelism to prevent an awkward construction. The series describing this "job" consists of phrases that begin "taking," "delivering" and "making sure." In situations where one phrase is longer than the others, the long phrase works best at the end of the sentence to preserve the sense of parallelism.

Guarantee of Excellence

Now to learn the distinguishing mark of all excellent writing, from memos to novels—sentence variety. This section and the next two will

introduce the idea of sentence variety. However, only one way exists for you to learn it—practice.

The first type of variety, length, is easy to understand. If you are like the overwhelming number of memo and letter writers, nearly all of your sentences are about two lines long, approximately 19 words. Such monotony is boring. Readers, while they will not be able to tell you the problem is sentence variety, will complain that the writing does not hold their attention. Use the occasional short sentence. Writing, even though read silently, is still always heard with the inner ear that seeks the musical rhythm of sentence variety.

Buried somewhere in your grade school memory is mention of a second type of variety, sentence structure: simple, compound and complex. These three structures are the foundation of language. Usually they are covered in a grammar course listing a bunch of rules set out as equally necessary to memorize. Sentence structure deserves better. To know these basic structures is to know how readers think.

The third type of sentence variety is timing, rarely taught in any school. Look carefully at the upcoming examples to see why "strung along" and "periodic" sentences produce different rhythms. Some memo and letter writers never use the periodic sentence. Again, the result is monotony.

The one-page essay on sentence variety (on Page 112) shows how to use variety. Examine the essay for examples of the three types of variety.

Fast Tips for revising
9. Refer to your reader by name.
10. Change a word ending in "ion" to a shorter one.
11. Cut "very," "rather" and "quite."

For most people, the idea of sentence variety will be entirely new. As we discussed earlier, it is not vocabulary that makes effective writing. Simple word substitutions do not make your thoughts more clear to the reader. Structure and organization do.

Now for your guarantee. If you master sentence variety, people will acknowledge you as an excellent writer. Your readers will not necessarily be able to say why they like your writing but they will finish your memos, letters and reports. By mastery I mean the ability to write with variety without thinking about it, adopting a natural, easy sense of rhythm that keeps the reader interested. It takes about three to five years of work. The result is worth the effort.

Sentence Variety

For lively, expressive writing, in business or out, vary sentences in three ways: length, structure and timing.

Length: Short, Medium or Long

While no universally recognized measure of length exists, the following definitions are useful guidelines.

Short   Less than one typewritten line.
Long   More than two typewritten lines.
Medium   Between short and long.

Structure: Simple, Compound or Complex

Simple   One independent clause with subject and verb expressing a complete thought.
    Example: The girls left early and played tag.

Compound   Two or more independent clauses each with a subject and a verb and both expressing complete thoughts.
    Example: We are almost done but we are waiting for Fred.

Complex   An independent clause joined with one or more dependent clauses; a dependent clause contains a subject and verb (like the independent clause) but does not express a complete thought.
    Example: We will be done when Fred gets here.

Timing: Strung Along or Suspended

Most sentences are "strung along," consisting of a basic thought with phrases added to the front or back. "Suspended" sentences, however, interrupt the basic thought, suspending interest until the thought is completed. In the examples below, the basic thought is underlined.

Strung along:	<u>Sales were up</u>, increasing profits, adding to bonuses and making the president happy. After cleaning up, <u>we will go home happy</u>.
Suspended:	<u>The project</u>, although it was delayed, <u>is more successful than we thought</u>. <u>The department</u>, however organized, <u>must function</u>.

Sentence Variety Keeps Readers Interested

People often say the writing they see at work is "boring" or "wordy." Long sentences and rambling paragraphs certainly contribute to such a judgment. Yet there is another reason so many memos, letters and reports lull a reader to sleep. They have no rhythm.

Constant repetition of sentence structure, which is what we find in most writing at work, causes people to lose interest. Monotony, besides being boring, is unnatural. Life changes; patterns vary. Music progresses through different chords. We vary the foods we eat at meals. Nobody gets excited about a parade composed entirely of high school marching bands and nothing else.

The same is true in writing. By using an unpredictable succession of different sounding sentences, effective writing holds our interest from one line to the next, sometimes even when it must labor under the disadvantage of routine content. Readers crave variety. Even when reading silently, people "hear" the sounds of writing, the rhymes, the euphonious words, and the sentence patterns. They may not consciously be able to explain the difference between a compound clause and a complex one. They may not be able to identify a strung along or suspended sentence. Their "inner ear," however, catches the rhythm and progress that comes from mixing in all types of sentences. Interest is maintained because the reader, never knowing what to expect next, continues to move forward to discover what the writer has to say.

Too often a memo consists of a loose series of simple and compound sentences, each about two lines long. No complex sentences. No suspended sentences. No short sentences. This unbroken pattern, which provides the reader with a sensation similar to eating the same food at every meal, causes people to grow bored and lose interest.

So what should we do? Every writing situation is different, of course, but we can identify a useful benchmark. In a one-page memo, which is a typical working document, we should see at least two periodic sentences. Four or five sentences should run less than one line. No more than two should run over four lines (unless there is a special circumstance). And two to five sentences should follow complex structure.

How does your writing compare to this benchmark?

11.
Sensible Mechanics Without a Bunch of Useless Theories and Rules

Usage Overview

This chapter presents the most common problems people have with punctuation and grammar. These are the questions that people ask me, and the problems I see at work. Neither you nor I know all the rules of language. Few people do–maybe nobody. We don't need to know them. What we need to know is how to quickly handle the little mechanical problems that arise during writing, so we can return to our real goal: enjoying ourselves at work.

Remember, all the work we have done so far. So often, when I reach this point in the writing workshops, people forget about swinging naturally. Instead, they once again become the sixth grader who so ardently tried to master the rules. If you are prepared when you write (answer the Eight Questions), if you know your process, and if you express yourself naturally, you will rarely even think about rules. On occasion, however, you may ask yourself whether or not you need to add a comma. This set of rules answers the question 99 percent of the time.

A comprehensive list of language rules, which would answer the last one percent of the questions, is too cumbersome to be useful. Besides, you can find that sort of list in many places. Only here, can you find a presentation of rules organized to solve the common problems of people writing at work. This set of rules is not about theories of language. It is about people, and their real problems. First comes a prelude of the chapter, a brief recitation of the major themes.

A Quick Look at the Rules

- Comma sparingly.
- Place comma after long introductory phrases.
- Use comma for direct address and titles.
- Don't use comma with double verbs.
- Put comma after conjunction in compound sentence.
- Put period and comma inside quotation marks.
- Use semicolons for compound sentences and long lists.
- Use colons to introduce.
- Maintain number agreement with subject/verb and noun/pronoun.
- Avoid dangling modifiers.
- Keep modifiers close to what they describe.
- Put hyphen in modifiers and not after "ly" words.
- Remember dashes, parentheses and ellipses are nutty.
- Capitalize formal titles only.
- Use "who" for people and "whom" for nothing.
- Remember "that" is more important than "which."
- Keep ideas parallel.
- Be positive.
- Beware of sentences beginning "it" or "there."
- Spell out numbers one to nine.
- If possible, substitute "since" or "because" for "as."
- Contract words to sound more personal.

- Use "8 p.m.," not "8:00 p.m."
- Consult chart for apostrophe problems.
- Obey all rules unless you have a clear reason not to.

Grammar and Punctuation: The Real Problem

How often has a discussion of writing at your job drifted far from the subject of the writing to dwell on punctuation or parts of speech? If your work is typical, this discussion has happened too often.

Usually the frustrations of writing are not about content; they are about mechanics, such as where to put the commas. Nothing destroys the joy of writing faster than getting mired in the mechanics. Grammar and punctuation—here grouped under the heading of usage—get in the way of writing because people expect too much of the mechanics. Yes, correct usage, like proper spelling, is necessary for getting the message across successfully. Mistakes draw attention to themselves and away from the action you want to accomplish.

The central role of mechanics also, unfortunately, has been a major cause of confusion for some writers who believe that memorizing the rules of usage is the path to readable, effective writing. In fact, knowing the rules of mechanics is not even necessary for effective writing. Look no farther than the nearest five year old. The child can communicate successfully, using complete sentences. Yet no five year old has the slightest understanding of the rules of usage. The same applies to adult writers: if you can talk without thinking about commas, you can write without thinking about commas. Concentrating on usage mechanics while writing is like thinking about your feet when you dance. It doesn't work. You have to dance to the music and write to the reader. Thinking harder about the mechanics helps neither your reader nor your dance partner.

The real problem of usage is the amount of time it takes to talk about it. The classic time waster is the discussion of whether to put a comma someplace or not. Either get on with it or, if punctuation has become so important, rephrase the sentence. Reviewing a few simple rules, most of which you have probably already encountered somewhere else, will help you save time writing.

The opening page of this section lists 20 rules that solve most writing problems at work. Any number of books on grammar and punctuation will give you the works if you want them. What I have found, however, is that knowing more rules only causes more confusion because you are always trying to apply rules instead of conveying meaning. The list of 20 is a handy guide for most problems. Now here is a more detailed explanation of what the rules mean.

Parts of Speech and Other Terms

If you want to brush up on the terms used in this section, take a look at these definitions. You may know this part so you can feel free to skip it.

You don't have to know any of this. You already understand how the language works. Writing naturally (especially after you practice the exercises in this book) is more valuable than writing to meet all rules.

"Usage" is the term I use to mean both "grammar" and "punctuation." Let's briefly define each of these words. Grammar is the forms and structures of words. Punctuation separates sentences and sentence elements. You can find more elaborate definitions, if you wish, in a dictionary or a book of usage.

Verb: an action word, taking many forms

Example: sit, to sit, sitting, sat, will sit

For a complete explanation of active and passive verbs, see Chapter Five. A special kind of verb to be familiar with is the verb of being. The verb "to be" is neither active nor passive. That goes for all of its forms, "is, "was," "will be," "might be" and the others.

Noun: person, place, action or thing as well as the less tangible quality, idea and state

Example: John loves Mary and sports.

"John" is a noun, subject of the sentence. "Mary" and "sports" are both nouns, objects of the verb love.

Modifier: a word that applies to other words; it never stands alone

Example: "good job"

The adjective "good" modifies the noun "job."

Example: "moving slowly"

The adverb "slowly" modifies the verb "moving."

1. adjectives modify nouns and pronouns; they denote quality, indicate number and make distinctions.
2. adverbs modify verbs, adjectives or other adverbs; they express relation of manner or quality, place, time, degree, number, cause, opposition, affirmation or denial; they often end in "ly." (The author does not like adverbs.)

Pronoun: a substitute for a noun

Example: Mary loves him, too.

The pronoun "him" is a substitute for the noun "John." (The author is kind of cranky about pronouns, too.)

You know it when you see it: "he," she," "it," "which," "that" and others.

Preposition: combines with a noun or pronoun to create a phrase

Example: with pay

The preposition "with" combines with the noun "pay" to create a phrase.

They are the little, dinky words (except for a couple) such as "of," "with," "for" and others.

Article: a sound with no meaning

There are three of them, "a," "an" and "the." Avoid relying on articles to carry meaning. Take them out of any sentence, and the sentence will still make sense but it will sound funny.

This simplified list gives you enough information to understand the following section. Grammar can be considerably more complex. For example, a whole group of words may function as a noun. You don't need to understand any of this to be a good writer. You can dance without knowing the names of each dance step.

For practice, identify the parts of the following sentence. The correct identification is at the end of this chapter.

The tall man walked quickly down the street by himself.

Two Systems of Punctuation

Few people realize the English language has two systems of punctuation. I didn't know it until I had to study up before giving my first writing workshop. This arcane tidbit is worth knowing because the conflict of the systems actually causes problems in the workplace. This is also the sort of thing that impresses people. But I don't recommend the information for that reason because the impressed ones always turn out to be the wrong people. First, let's look at each of the systems.

Open or rhetorical

This system assigns value to each punctuation mark on the basis of timing.

comma:	1 count
semicolon:	2 counts
colon, dash:	3 counts
period, question:	4 counts.

Closed

This system, the more common one, depends on the connection of sentence parts.

The open system is used for speeches. The closed system is the one most people are familiar with. The problem comes when one person *listens* to how a sentence sounds and wants to add a comma while another person *looks* at the parts and wants to leave the comma out. Both persons are right. Once you realize the discussion is about the two different systems, you can reach agreement.

Comma Sparingly

The "serial comma" causes more problems than any other mechanical detail. It applies to a series of three or more items (word or phrases).

The flag is red, white and blue.

In the sentence above, there is no comma separating "white" from "and." Most experts now say that a serial comma in this situation is not necessary. Some grammar specialists, however, say the comma should go in; otherwise, the list consists of only two items. In this case, they say, the two items are the color "red" and the color "white and blue." Either way is correct. Just don't waste time thinking about it. I recommend using as few punctuation marks as possible so I drop the comma.

One instance can cause problems. When writing a legal document, it is safest to include the serial comma so that there cannot be the least possibility of confusion. The classic example, though not likely one you will use, involves a will. If a will states, "A, B and C" divide the estate equally," the lawyer for person A will contend that his client should receive half as the equal division.

Although it is more efficient drop the comma in most instances, sometimes you may want to include the serial comma in longer phrases.

She is planning the schedule, filling out payroll, and making assignments for next week.

Another common use for the comma is to separate "long" introductory clauses. The following two sentences are correct.

After finishing the last requirement, we will be done.

After finishing we will leave.

The phrase "after finishing" is not separated from the rest of the sentence because it is "short." Usually any introductory phrase longer than four or five words calls for a comma.

Other uses for the comma are for direct address—when you call someone by name—or titles.

As you can see, Bill, we have a growing problem.

Direct your calls to Mary Conover, day supervisor.

When you get tired of using the word "but," you may want to use "however." Separate it by commas.

The second option, however, will be more useful.

Several other words, used in a certain way the beginning or end of a sentence, are set apart by a comma.

Let's eat the pie, too.

Again, dinner started late.
Instead, we settled for one dessert.

A common way of attributing information is to use an "according to" construction. Separate it with a comma.

The department works well, according to the manager.

According to the field reports, we're done.

Use a comma in dates and for cities.

The best date is Friday, April 10.

I'll see you in St. Louis, Missouri.

Commas and No Commas

Compound sentences (see Chapter 10) often hold together on a conjunction. Some call for commas, some don't. Here is one that does.

I am working hard, and I am happy.
Also: or, but, nor, for

Not: then, yet, thus, so, since, because
Example: We are going to the zoo because it is a fun place.

There is a difference of opinion on putting "so" and "yet" in the list of words that do not take the comma. Again, I recommend avoiding punctuation when possible.

Restrictive or Non-Restrictive

In the previous chapter, you learned about using compound sentences to create sentence variety. That's good because now we are going to talk about restrictive and non-restrictive sentences, a confusing topic on any account but impossible until you understand compound sentences. Look at the following sentences. Note that one has a comma in the middle and the other doesn't.

People who live in glass houses should not throw stones. (restrictive)

The lawnmower, which is green, is in the garage. (non-restrictive)

Why the difference? The first sentence is restrictive. That means the clause "who live in glass houses" restricts the meaning of houses to a certain type of houses. When you use a restrictive sentence, that means the clause is necessary. So remember *restrictive, necessary, no comma.*

In the second sentence, it is not necessary to know what color the lawn mower is to know where it is. So the clause is not necessary, making it non-restrictive. The commas indicate that you can remove the phrase or clause, and the essential meaning of the sentence remains intact.

If you are getting a headache, that's okay. This is probably the toughest concept in the book. It's worth thinking about and practicing until you understand it.

Quotation Marks

Commas and periods always go inside the quotation marks. Always. It looks funny to some people (not me) but it's a universal rule.

He said, "Let's go."

"Let's go," he said.

The report, called "quarterly 2," will be done soon.

The other stuff that ends a sentence, question marks and exclamation points, goes in or out of the quotation marks, depending on the meaning of the sentence. Look at these two examples.

Did she say, "Let's go"?

She said, "Why go?"

Don't worry so much about this last part. If you can't handle it easily and naturally when you write, write the sentence differently to eliminate a punctuation problem. "Just don't waste time thinking about it!"

This is good time to mention the difference between direct and indirect quotes. The direct quote is separated by a comma. The indirect quote has no comma but does have the word "that."

She said, "We can go now."

She said that we can go now.

Quotes are powerful. Few people use them. But because they are credible, they add strength to your work. Find out exactly what the boss or the customer said and put it in quotes.

Double Verbs

Take a look at these two sentences.

He goes to school during the day and works at night.

The manager sets the plan, and the supervisor implements it.

Both are punctuated correctly. One has a comma before the "and." The other doesn't. Why? In the first sentence, two verbs work off one subject. He "goes" and the same he "works." In the second sentence, two subjects do two different actions. Manager "sets." Supervisor "implements." When one subject works on both verbs, no comma. Two different subjects working on two different verbs are separated by a comma. The all too common problem I see is that writers add a comma in the first type of sentence. You can tell what that does. The reader sees the comma and begins to look for the next subject. The next subject never comes so the reader gets confused. This is a good one to check for during your revision stage.

Semicolons, Love 'Em or Leave 'Em

If you don't want to use semicolons, don't. And feel good about it. If you are wondering about semicolons, this section answers the major questions. The most frequent use for semicolons is when you cramp two sentences together. Like this.

> She is vice president of finance; he is vice president of human resources.

The part before the semicolon stands on its own as a complete sentence. So does the part after the sentence. Complete sentences—that's the key to semicolons. So you ask, "Why not just use two sentences?" You can. The writer uses a semicolon when two sentences are close in meaning or when they are short and parallel.

Often at work you list long phrases. Normally such phrases are separated by commas. However, when commas fall inside the phrases to be separated by still more commas, your reader can be confused. Use a semicolon to keep things straight.

> The officers are Fred Smith, chair; Mary Chin, vice chair; Ramona Rosario, treasurer; and Bill Johnson, secretary.

Introducing the Colon

The colon introduces something else, usually a list. Here is the way I like to use the colon.

These are the reasons why we should do it:
1. I like it;
2. You like it;
3. It is free, and
4. It is easy.

The term for this format is "tabular." There are several varieties. Note how each item is numbered. Items are separated by a semicolon because they are complete sentences. The "and" falls at the end of the third item, not the beginning of the last item. You can also use bullets instead of numbers. When the items are not complete sentences, do not use semicolons.

The colon is also used in a way similar to a semicolon. The two parts are closely connected.

I'll tell you why not: it's dumb.

This is another rule that does not enjoy university agreement. The colon is going through a change. The old rule was that the first word of the sentence following the colon is capitalized. Again, if you want to stay with the old rules, fine.

Number Agreement

You already know that sentence subjects must agree in number with their verbs, and pronouns must agree with the nouns they substitute for. This reminder is for other people because I still see this problem.

NO
The committee stayed on their agenda.
The group set their course.
Every student must find their own writing process.

YES

The committee stayed on its agenda.

Committee members stayed on their course.

NO

The resources of each area is defined below.

Attached for your review are a list of major duties.

YES

The resources are defined.

A list is attached.

These pronouns are all singular: each, every, no one, nobody, everyone, everybody, anyone, anybody, someone, somebody.

Dangling Modifiers

Take a look at the next two sentences. Find what is wrong.

NO

After looking at the choices, the best idea was clear.

Using the given figures, it will be necessary to decide on quality assurance.

Each sentence has a word that is supposed to describe something but there is nothing to describe. You have probably heard of "dangling modifiers." In the first sentence, no is "looking"; in the second sentence, no one is "using." Add people to correct the problem.

YES

After looking at the choices, we clearly saw the best idea.

It will be necessary for someone to use the given figures to decide quality assurance.

NO
Please look at the description of the department which is attached.

YES
Please look at this department description.

Vague Pronouns

All too common. Take a look.

The manager told the director he was wrong.

Who is wrong, the manager or the director? We can't tell. Rewrite the sentence.

We have problems. This is bad.

Beware of sentences beginning "This." As in this example, the word often refers to nothing in particular. The writer is referring only to a vague notion in his or her mind, unstated on paper.

Pronouns also must come after the noun they refer to. Otherwise, a guessing reader is left confused.

Because we are doing them differently this year and they will take longer, we will begin the annual reports this week.

Hyphens

Most hyphen problems at work will be solved by the following example.

He works full time.
He has a full-time job.

When "full time" stands alone, no hyphen. When it describes something, hyphen. Same goes with "part time."

Here is the hyphen rule: If you can apply the first word to the last word and the phrase makes sense the way you mean it, no hyphen. These two examples show how the rule works.

computer generated picture

one-year-old baby

The hyphen also connects phrases that describe another word. In the following example, the first five words together describe the word "kind."

one-day-at-a-time kind of person

Sometimes the hyphen hangs out there by itself. It is actually a useful technique to save words in a sentence. You can see how it works in this example.

10-and 20-year plans

Never hyphen after an "ly" word. Yech!

Dash, Parentheses & Ellipsis

Again, as with the semicolon, if you don't want to think about these three eccentric relatives of the punctuation family, don't. But I'm writing a reference chapter so I have to put them in.

The dash is used for abrupt changes. While it may look like a hyphen, it is longer. Word processing programs usually contain a way to type a dash. On a typewriter, the dash is made by striking two hyphens in a row.

The director—he never recovered from the embarrassment at the conference—will be there.

The parenthesis is used for unnecessary information. I think of it as a whisper. Readers often skip parenthetical material.

Sales presentations (especially in the afternoon) should be as brief as possible.

Parentheses always come in pairs. Eliminate the single parenthesis after a number in a list. Use a period.

The three dots, called an ellipsis, denote something is missing. They are used within quoted material. Only three. The three dots are treated as a word, with a space before and after. When they fall at the end of a sentence, the period becomes a fourth dot. A string of dots is sometimes thrown in by confused writers to indicate a pause or to imply a question. The technique only confuses. Here is a correct use of the thing.

"In 1930 they did...not today."

Capitals

These examples demonstrate the two most frequent situations where capitulation problems arise.

Department of Finance and Administration
    but: finance department

Capitalize the official title but not the unofficial one.

Vice President Debbie Amundsen
    but: Debbie Amundsen, vice president

Yes, you do not capitalize the title after a name. Nearly every place where I have worked or I have provided training, people capitalize the title after the name. So what, I don't care. I just don't want to waste time talking about it.

I include the rule because it is a useful one. Memos often contain lists of people and their positions. So many capital letters are hard to read.

People Who

Lately, I've been seeing this pronoun problem all over. People write like this.

NO
The managers that matter are here.

People are always "who," never "that."

YES
The managers who matter are here.

By the way, never use the word "whom." It bugs people. Even if you use it correctly, people think about. Write around it. (Don't tell your English teacher I said that.)

That Is Important

Using which and that is confusing (at least for me). When in doubt, write around it. If you really must know the rule, here it is. Use "that" to begin clauses necessary for the complete meaning of the sentence. Use "which" for extra stuff you are throwing in. (However, "which" can go both ways, if it has too. See the section on restrictive clauses.)

Identify and master a writing process that works best for you.

Writing at work, which you now do better than before, is usually required for most jobs.

Part of the problem is that "that" is a word that can be used so many ways. The best approach is not to think about it. Most people, writing naturally, use correct grammar without reciting the rules to themselves as they compose. Thinking about rules confuses people because they feel a need to be able to state them precisely. They don't. Rules came about after humans invented writing, not before.

Keep Words, Phrases and Clauses Parallel

This guideline is discussed in detail in Chapter Ten.

Be Positive

More than a handy comment about attitude, be positive is an admonition to write about what is there rather than what isn't.

NO
I am not saying we shouldn't do the project

Huh? What are you saying?

YES
I have reservations about doing this project.

Beware of Sentences Beginning "It" or "There."

While it is not strictly incorrect to begin a sentence with either of these two words, such sentences are often unclear, passive statements with little human involvement. At your revision stage, examine them carefully.

NO
It was decided that weekly reports were most effective.

YES
The management committee decided weekly reports were most effective.

Spell Out Numbers One to Nine

We have eight offices and a management staff of 11.

If Possible, Substitute "Since" or "Because" for "As."

"As," like "that," is a pain because it performs too many roles (can we get our money back from whoever sold us this language?). Many uses of "as" are correct. Don't change them. One is a horrible-sounding mess. The way to tell is this: If you can take out the "as" and plug in either "since" or "because" and the sentence makes sense, do it. Now the example part.

NO
We should leave now as we are ready.

YES
We should leave now because we are ready.

YES
Work as quickly as possible.

The Right Form of the Possessive, or Where does the Apostrophe Go?

The following rules show how to use the apostrophe correctly in the possessive form. Rules are arranged in order of most common application. Once you find a rule that applies to your problem, forget the others. When you face a problem, read Rule 1. If it solves your problem, don't bother with the rest. If it does not fit your situation precisely, go to the next rule.

1. Form the possessive singular of most nouns by adding *'s*.

Bill's   watch's   woman's rights

2. Do the same thing when the noun ends in a double *s*.

the boss's idea

3. Proper nouns ending in s, add only the *'*.

Dickens' novels   Charles' job

(Note: This rule disagrees with Strunk and White.)

4. Plural nouns ending in s, add only the '.
the firms' presidents   the watches' springs

5. Plural nouns not ending in s, add '*s*.
women's rights

6. Nouns ending the same in singular and in plural, treat as plural.
two deer's tracks (Rule 5)
one corps' location (Rule 4)

7. Joint possessives use an ' only after the last word.
Bill and Mary's department
(two people in the same department)

8. For individual possession of more than one, both have '.
Bill's and Mary's time sheets
(two people, two time sheets)

Other Uses of the Apostrophe

Indicate a missing letter.
it's = it is   who's = who is   you're = you are

For plural of letters (rare)
P's and Q's

Not for possessive pronouns
mine, ours, your, yours, his, hers, its, their, whose

Contract Words to Sound More Personal.

Especially useful at times are these words: can't, you're, let's, and won't. Classical writing instructors hate it when I recommend contractions. But they're most personable tone fits the modern, human-relations-intensive work style. If you don't want to sound informal, do not use contractions.

Correct: 8 p.m. and 8:15 p.m. or 8 P.M. and 8:15 P.M.

The first, a lower case "p.m.," is preferred. Include the periods for now, but this is an example of where the punctuation mark is being used less and less. Incorrect: 8:00 p.m.

Parts of the Sentence Example from Page 147:

The tall man walked quickly down the street by himself.

The	article
tall	adjective modifier
man	noun
walked	verb
quickly	adverb modifier
down	preposition
the	article
street	noun (part of prepositional phrase with "down")
by	preposition
himself	pronoun substituting for "man"

12.
Public Relations for the Shy

Public Relations Writing

From time to time, organizations without a formal public relations office decide to send out a news release. Unlike several public relations functions, which can be surprisingly complicated, the news release is most efficiently handled in-house without hiring someone from the outside. To be effective, however,. a news release must meet certain professional standards that news people expect.

The usual cause for failure of a news release is not poor writing. It is lack of news. Too many news releases contain nothing more than self-congratulatory material of little interest to the wider public. By directing your message to the wider news audience, you will produce a news release that is more likely to be printed or to attract the attention of a reporter who will write a story.

For the majority of purposes, news releases fall into one of three categories:

1. Routine Information

Examples: Personnel changes, public financial information (such as year-end information required by government agencies), meeting or event notices, other minor announcements.

2. Publicity Announcement

Examples: Introduction of new product or service, interesting change for existing product or service, anniversary, new sales campaign, fund raising campaign, event sponsorship, contribution to the community.

3. Spontaneous News Announcement

Examples: Response to crisis or emergency, comment on news developments elsewhere, response to multiple reporter calls, get a jump on unfavorable news coming out shortly.

Like any memo or letter, a news release must get to the point right away. Especially in the case of a meeting notice, all information necessary for a person to get to the meeting must be in the first paragraph.

Do not feel a need to write like a professional or to be especially clever. In fact, the writing (or "copy" in news jargon) is less important than format or distribution.

A sample format follows. For distribution, it is worth the extra time and effort to call the news outlets in advance to get the exact name, title and address of the news editors and to keep the mailing list up to date. Otherwise use a phone directory.

In the following passage is a public service announcement. Non-profit organizations and government agencies submit PSA's to radio stations. They are like plain commercials you don't pay for. Broadcasters have different policies. Some don't run them. Some want printed scripts for their announcers to read on the air. Some want taped announcements.

As with any public relations project, you must know what the news media wants and plan accordingly. Most public relations projects fail. That's because people plunge into doing them without first thinking through a mass communication strategy. You won't find the strategy in this book either. We are concentrating on the writing aspect of public relations only.

NEWS RELEASE ON LETTERHEAD
OR SHEET MARKED "NEWS"

Contact: Owen Topp, division manager, 555-2222
Photo or Video Opportunity: YES (NO for meeting notice)

RELEASE: Month Day, Year

HEADLINE SUMMARIZES SUBJECT

A news release gets to the point immediately with factual information about an event (not an idea). Meeting notices include in the first paragraph all information necessary to get to the meeting. Cleverness is okay if it works. Avoid such cuteness as puns with no bearing on the subject of the release.

Give information clearly in a natural style. Do not feel a need to "write like a professional." Use third person, not second (you) or first (we).

Short sentences and simple words are strongest. Double space, indent paragraphs, and use one side of the paper. When announcing a new service or product, include the name of a person making the announcement, not just a faceless organization. Double check names, numbers and quotes.

Put background information about your organization after the primary news announcement. The LEB123S format is most effective.

Be prepared to talk to a reporter who has follow up questions. At the end, just stop.

###

PSA ON LETTERHEAD

Public Service Announcement
Start Date: Month Day, Year
Kill Date: Month Day, Year
Length: 30 seconds

Contact: Name, title, phone number

<u>Headline for Subject Only</u>

Come to an exciting event for people just like you at this place and time. All the information you need to do what we want you to do comes right away—including specific time and date and exact location.

Here is a clever or memorable statement about the event, campaign or action we want you to take.

This is a brief final reminder of the action, possibly the date.

Good-bye if there is time.

Newsletters

On occasion, you will be asked to write for a newsletter. We are not going to talk about editing and production—only writing. Since you already know the LEB123S format, you know how to write for your newsletter.

To be effective, you also need to know the deadline for giving your *copy* (the writing that goes into a printed document) to the editor and the date of publication.

The biggest failing of newsletter stories is no news. People write generally about their company or club without focusing on actual events. Newsletters should more often be about events coming up rather than events past. So don't write about what already happened at last month's luncheon. Write about what is going to happen at next month's luncheon.

Include as many names of people as possible. Paint a picture. End with an action statement so readers can get involved.

Always hit your deadline, no matter what. If you don't hit the deadline, you don't have a newsletter. Sounds good, right? Not really. I have found that people hate deadlines. Most workplaces talk deadlines and never meet them. Something "comes up." When writing for the newsletter, something almost always "comes up." For this reason, most organizations should not put out newsletters. As a group of individuals, they are not capable of working together to meet a deadline, month in and month out. So I recommend a "bulletin" instead of a "newsletter." A bulletin comes out when it comes out. The name implies updated information, just like a newsletter. But it frees the staff from having to comply with a schedule it most likely is not going to meet. Face reality in the beginning. Get it out when it comes out. Don't promise monthly issues unless you know you will always publish on schedule even if "something comes up."

Brochures

The first two rules on brochures are:

1. Don't do a brochure. People rarely read them.

2. If you have to do a brochure, pay a professional thousands of dollar to do it right.

You almost certainly will not take my advice. So write a brochure in the AIDA format. Heavy on emotion, light on facts. We don't need to know everything about your product or service from reading the brochure. We just want to feel good about. Good enough to stay interested.

The purpose of a brochure is to stimulate action. Usually that is to make a phone call or to come in. You can't sell something from a brochure. Don't try. So focus on why your reader will call or come in. Describe benefits, not features. Use pictures.

If you use the standard 8 1/2" by 11" paper with two folds, use the first panel to attract the reader's attention. For the first two inside panels, keep your reader's interest by providing factual information. In the third panel appeal to emotion. On the back (left panel as you fold it out), list and overcome possible objections. On the back panel (in the middle as you fold it out), describe the action you want the reader to take. Make sure the phone number is easy read. Say something plain, clear and strong like "Call today."

13.
Action Summary

Determine your own process for writing successfully

Recognize the writing styles at your work place

Research your subject

Know your audience

Use simple, direct language

Write for action

Express your personal style naturally

Revise after you write

Plan for approvals

When you master the fundamentals, go faster

Final Exercises

1. SOLVE PROBLEMS

Identify three possible writing problems. They don't have to be your own problems. Write a strategy to solve each one. In a paragraph describe new techniques you have learned to solve the problem. If you do not have a complete strategy for a solution, describe where you will look to find a solution.

2. IDENTIFY YOUR OWN STYLE

Describe in your own words what your writing style is. Maybe that has to do with your choice or words or your choice of topics. Maybe it is the way you begin or a particular greeting you use in letters. Capture it on paper. Extend the "my writing process" exercise from the book. Instead of a few comments, list everything about your own style. You can also list what is not yet in your style but you want it in.

3. CHART YOUR COURSE

What are you going to do to improve your writing skills or to maintain them at the level you feel makes them a building block to success in your career? Write it down. If it's not on paper, it doesn't exist (unless it's on TV). Good luck.

Epilogue

For up to date information about writing at work and other types of writing to get work done, see www.dolan2000.com.

About the Author

Michael Dolan is a public relations consultant and trainer who has taught 1000s of managers and others to write better. He has offered his writing for action workshops for both businesses and government agencies—large and small. A former news reporter and magazine writer, he has published in several national periodical. He created The Public Involvement Network, one of the first Internet sites for professional development. He lives and writes in Portland, Oregon.

Appendix I

Sample responses

The following pages contain these sample responses to exercises in the text:

1. Sample responses to reader point of view from Chapter 2.

2. Sample Memo from exercise on Chapter 4.

3. Passive to Active possible responses from Chapter 5.

4. Talkability Exercise possible responses from Chapter 7.

Reader Point of View

1. Please answer all the questions on this form. That way we can fill your order as fast as possible.

or

If you answer all the questions on this form, you will get your order faster.

2. You can always depend on us for excellent service. Your order will always be processed as quickly as possible. Not only can you choose

from the widest selection in the business, but you can also visit us at convenient locations all over town.

or

We serve you faster than anyone in the business. You can choose from the largest selection of stock in town. And our stores are located conveniently close to you.

3. Your payday schedule is changing to the first and third Friday of each month. You will be paid on the fourth Friday of this month under the old schedule. The new schedule begins with your paycheck on the first Friday of next month. If you have questions, your office manager can give you more information.

or

From now on, you will receive your paycheck on the first and third Friday of the month rather than the second and fourth Friday. That means your next paycheck will cover one week instead of the usual two weeks. If you have a question, see your office manager.

4. You will be pleased to know the project is going well. The other department managers have approved most of your recommendations. We will probably complete the project by the deadlines set at last month's meeting.

or

Most of the recommendations in your memo were approved by the other managers. You will be pleased to know the project is going well. The project will probably be completed by the deadline.

Natural Manufacturing Company
office memorandum

TO: Marketing staff and finance staff

            List below

FROM: Leslie Morley *L S*

SUBJECT: Unlocked supply room

DATE: Month Day, Year

1 Members of the marketing and finance departments are going to have to change the way we use our supply room. The door to the room was again found unlocked early this morning by the security guard.

2 The same thing happened last month. We cannot tell if anything was stolen in these two incidents. But the company has been going through more supplies than usual lately. I know many people have been working long hours lately and although we have no reason for alarm I want to make sure we are taking the usual precautions.

3 Only the staffs on this floor regularly use the supply room. I have talked with Lewis Cannon and B.N. Counter, finance manager, about this security problem. This floor may lose its supply room if we are not more careful.

4 The best solution is for everyone on the floor to take better care of the supply room starting today. I do not think it is a good idea to establish an elaborate security system with all kinds of rules; but that is always an option.

5 From now on, please make sure the supply room is always locked after 5 p.m. even if you are still here working late. If you want to work late

and do not have a key, see your office manager. Double check the door when you leave.

Distribution list: Elizabeth Morales, Bill Chen, Harold Square, Nwusi Askari, Connie Delta, Jan Dempsey, Chip Sahoy.

Copies: Lewis Cannon, B.N. Counter, Security office

Comments on the Stockroom Memo

The writer wants to begin with "you." However, since the memo is about a problem, Leslie does not want to strike an accusatory tone. She achieves the "you" tone by identifying the readers. The writer states the impact on the reader first but still gets the latest information – last night's incident – into the first paragraph.

The second paragraph explains why the issue matters. With a second report from security, we have a trend, not an isolated incident. The situation may explain higher costs. This budgeting information is probably not something the reader already knows.

Anticipating the impact on the reader, Leslie acknowledges the people who are working hard. The writer here lets the reader know that security precautions extend to something the reader is interested in, personal security.

Paragraph three sets out some facts that support the first sentence. It answers the question about what communication has taken place in the past: a conversation among the three mangers. This sets the memo in the flow of daily business, instead of making it look like an isolated message from the boss. Note that the marketing manager does not just blame the vice president for the possible loss of the stockroom but sends the message in a supportive way. A problem is immediately followed with the solution: "be more careful." The writer sees no need to tell readers what is in the stockroom because they already know that.

Instead of surveying all the possible options for a response, in paragraph four, Leslie zeros in on the one option we are following now. However, the writer has answered what communication may happen in the future. If this casual plan does not work, the next memo may introduce "an elaborate security system." If so, the readers are prepared for the message.

With the foundation of facts and reader point of view in place, the reader is now ready to hear—and act on—the action statement. Paragraph five is a series of simple statements in direct form. The reader knows precisely what the writer wants. The list of specific actions directly flows from the general sentence that begins the memo.

Copies go to persons mentioned in the memo. Unlike the people mentioned in the "to" line, people getting copies are not expected to do the action in the final paragraph.

You may have written this memo with a different approach. That is fine. There are several worthwhile approaches. You may have moved immediately to a new security system. You may have called a meeting. You could have focused more on security or more on supplies. The important thing is to answer the 8 questions. In this situation, as with many at work, we can see more than purpose. No matter what your purpose make sure to keep it from the beginning. Do not start out writing about supplies and switch half way through to a discussion of security.

Passive to Active

1. Too many people use the copier.

2. Neighbors and representatives of the water district raised several concerns at the September hearing.

3. We project the program will be complete in 2002.

   or

   The program will be complete in 2002.

4. Figure 2 shows the department's productivity and its characteristics.

5. Ground water and creeks in the area recharge the lake.

6. Taking college courses helps aspiring managers get promotions faster.

7. Hard work and diligence characterize people who achieve excellence.

Talkability Exercise

These sentences are correct responses to the talkability exercise on Page 97. They are not the only responses.

1. Look at new ways of doing things. The past does not control the future.
2. The way we are working now looks okay. So we don't a need to make changes just to comply with out-of-date forecasts.
3. When in Nome, do as the Nomans do. (Laugh a little, OK?)
4. Clear graphics help get your point across in large groups and small ones.
5. The best way to manage today is by using broad skills. We should not make the mistake of hiring someone who is very good at only one skill.
6. We will go faster if your people and my people blend their skills to work as a team.
7. She has all the skills needed to do the job. Yet I wonder how well she will get along with others. She most likely won't have a problem. I will watch her at first to make sure.
8. The common tests show we are doing as much as we can. This is an odd time, though. Keep a close watch to ensure that we use every resource we have to its fullest.

You may want to measure the readability (not my word) of your responses.

Appendix II

What Other People Liked

In Chapter 2, you wrote down what you liked in a memo, letter or report at work. Here is a list of the ideas people contributed in workshops when I asked them to write down what they liked. They follow no particular order. I offer them to you so you will have an idea of what your readers may be looking for.

consider audience, common language, short and concise, graphics and tables, make point early, unique format, humor (to the right audience), clear purposes that are stated early, succinct, titles, personal touch, maintains focus, prioritizes importance, simple language, positive, good use of punctuation, illustrate meaning, to the point,

truthful, points of reference, quotations, distribution list, pertinent information, facts, good spelling, punctuation and grammar, short paragraphs, active voice, assertive, information number, scanning ability (easy to read quickly),

what it means to me, subject line, name spelled correctly, affects the reader, timelines and deadlines stated, states action required, white space, expectations made clear, date including year, signed, sincere, clear, concise, appropriate humor, complete background, attachments when necessary, referrals attached, who all is involved, "please" and "thank you," follows an organized structure, logical progression of ideas, complete meeting information, clearances stated in memo, funding sources cited, all information needed to make it easy to act, legible, white space between paragraphs, readable type size, personal tone, audience defined, headings and bullets, what's going to happen now, short, not fancy, words, all questions raised and answered, quality paper, correct fonts,

spell out abbreviations, main points highlighted or underlined, color paper for urgent messages, colored graphics, electronic mail for fast responses, states whether the writer wants feedback,

introduction explains purpose, give command if no other choices, touch of humor, define consequences if action not taken, sent to appropriate worker at the workplace, get to them in reasonable time to respond, subject identified, proper tone with respect to the subject, relating to the job, states desired result, close with confidence.

Appendix III

Follow Up Resources

Dolan Management

http://www.dolan2000.com
mdolan@dolan2000.com
503-287-4876
1001 SW 5th Ave, STE 1100, Portland OR 97204

Professional Associations

Association for Business Communication, www.theabc.org

International Association of Business Communicators, www.iabc.com

Society for Technical Communication, www.stc.org

Women in Communication, www.womcom.org

Public Relations Society of America, www.prsa.org

Career Guides and Periodicals

Business Week's Guide to Careers, 1221 Avenue of the Americas, New York NY 10020

The Business Writer, 407 South Dearborn, Chicago IL 60605

Career Opportunity News, Garrett Park Press, Garrett Park MD 20896

Communications Briefings, 806 Westminister Blvd, Blackwood NJ 08012

Commerce Business Daily, US Government Printing Office, Washington DC, 20402-9371

Wall Street Journal, 200 Liberty St, New York NY 10281

Appendix IV

For Your Writing Library

Some books of interest. Check the web site for more information, dolan2000.com.

How to Write, Speak and Think More Effectively by Rudolf Flesch; New American Library, 1951. Fun and useful.

Language in Thought and Action by S.I. Hayakawa; Harcourt, Brace, Jovanovich, 1972. Readable study of what people think about when they communicate.

Write to Learn, by Donald Murray; Holt, Rinehart and Winston, 1984. Pleasant style, focus on process.

Business Report Writing, by Joel P. Bowman and Bernadine P. Branchaw; The Dryden Press, 1984. For all kinds of reports.

Writing with Power, by Peter Elbow; Oxford University Press, 1981.

Write for Results, by William D. Andrews and Deborah C. Andrews; Little, Brown, 1982.

Gregg Reference Manual (9th edition) by William Sabin; Gregg Division of McGraw-Hill, 2000. Practical and usable.

A Passage to India by E.M. Forster; Harcourt, Brace, World, 1952. Entertaining novel whose nicely drawn characters show the pitfalls of not understanding another's point of view.

References

"Damn it, Hopkins, didn't you get yesterday's memo?"

From *The New Yorker Magazine*
Permission is granted for: use in *Write Better and Get Ahead At Work*, 2000, by Michael Dolan, to be published by I Universe, 2000.

June 7, 2000

Index

Printed in the United States
130800LV00002B/1-18/A